For You, My Love

From,
Danielle Cassidy

Copyright © 2024 by Danielle Cassidy
All rights reserved.
No part of this publication may be reproduced, distributed, or transmitted in any form or by any means, including photocopying, recording, or other electronic or mechanical methods, without the prior written permission of the publisher, except as permitted by U.S. copyright law.

First edition, 2024
ISBN: 979-8-218-48760-7

A Poem Called "Summer-Land"

—Written originally in 2010—

In the park, where nothing is dark,
In the grass beneath a tree,
Where all of our secrets are to be seen,
That's where I lay at night to dream.

On your chest, that's where I lean,
Hearing your heart's gentle beating,
Seeing all there is to be seen,
Wrapped in your arms as our hearts gleam.

Love, that's all I see to live, for it's all I have to give.
It is what makes my life have the slightest glimmer,
As I sit in my room watching the water shimmer.
For, that is where the moon will shine,
And in my dreams… I am yours, and you become all mine.

The moon, the moon, that many associate with gloom—
To us it is the sun… the sun, beneath it is where we run.
The sea, the sea—won't you search for me?

Over the water, I see a spark.
The wind, singing to me as a lark:
'Across the sea is where you be,'
Waiting there beneath our safest lee.
I feel the earth and sand pulsing beneath my feet, begging me to see.

On the bluff is where we will meet.
Our love will ring,
Just as the doves will all sing.
Without regret… that's how we met.

So, under that tall ever-green tree,
That is our safest lee…
Where our fears can be shown and our lives can be born…
I beg you to tightly hold onto me—
We will not part.
For together we be, and forever it shall stay,
For we.

Written for my dearest <u>only</u> Love,
with the hope that these words will somehow find their way to you.
So we may find our way home.

My Love,

In this world, there are many realities.

We know this with a clarity some will likely always disbelieve, and find impossible. Yet, even while those who experience life similarly are hesitant to openly speak about it, because they fear being called "crazy" for seeing things differently—afraid they'll have to bear all that *you*'ve had to endure, by never hiding your truth—I still sincerely believe we aren't alone, not even remotely.

And, perhaps, one day it'll be easier to openly be *as* we are.

Perhaps, even those who just now find the thought impossible will soon open their minds with hope—maybe, writing this for you will help them, as well—and, maybe, they'll start to see what exists beyond the physical reality, too. The truth of our spirits. And, just how connected these worlds are: the balanced realities of the body, mind and spirit. Maybe, then the world will be more kind: understanding.

Knowing this beautiful, mysterious land as we do.

But, at this point in time, many only experience this reality in confused flashes they can barely hold onto after they wake. Images too strange or random to hold sense, that quickly fade in their memory. And, even when they experience the rare dreams where they feel more awake, seeing faces they know enough to recall, and scenes that almost make sense; even if the familiar faces remember, too; they eventually let them fade as the rest do, thinking them interesting or strange, but looking no further.

Just a strange occurrence that made some sense, but held no meaning.

It's only those like us—the true "dreamers" of the world—who know the truth of this reality, because we don't *dream*. We don't even really sleep. We simply close our eyes to one reality, and open them to another: the spiritual reality most *can* probably see, but don't trust their minds enough to. Because, it isn't just the beautiful world we all strive for, though it's definitely filled with love, hope, freedom and happiness… it's also all the things our spirits try to hide, when awake.

What we try to bury, hoping to forget and ignore.

All the things you and I have never had a choice *but* to face: always just as much a part of that reality as the waking one. Because, being apart is as impossible as living without breath. And, the only way we can find our way home—to one another—when we physically can't be, is to be together in spirit.

It was *you* who found a way to make it possible for us to stay always together, even in our separate worlds. And, while I know my words won't ever need any explanation, not to you, for those outside of our world who may also be reading them on their way *to* you, I'll try to explain this the best I can: how you and I truly live *two* lives, one as ourselves and one together; one in the reality all see, and one in the spiritual reality of dreams. Living our lives, in both worlds, *sharing* our realities with the other: hearing our entwined thoughts as though with one mind, seeing our divided visions as though with one set of eyes.

Constantly held in balance between the physical, and spiritual.

Seeing so much of the world, living two lives simultaneously, and yet never able to see the whole picture of the moments before us. Oftentimes, having the waking reality seem to pass by in a strange sort of a haze as we experience half of each life we walk, our spirit longing to be where the other is, but unable to find our way home. It's only when we are together that we may see everything—truly everything.

When we're side-by-side, and the other is safe beside us.

So, in this land of dreams, between the two of us we know every piece by heart. All of its beauty and secrets. Because, we see it as one being, rather than with split senses: hearing every sound, tasting every flavor, smelling every scent, and seeing every sight together, as we feel all the magnificent and powerful feelings those who exist only in the waking world will never really comprehend.

The touch of truly connecting with our spirit.

Here we can experience many weeks in a single night, making the waking day we must spend "parted" more bearable. And, though perhaps some will never understand, we know all the days that pass in this world are days we really have lived. Every hard fight we face, we really have fought. Every step we follow, we really did take. Every beautiful pleasure we know, we really do feel.

It's as you once said to me, "the depth of our connection allows us to be, even when we're thousands of miles apart, far closer than most standing side-by-side."

And, you made this yet more true, though you'll never accept the credit for it, by molding *our* world: it all started with a beautiful little sea of wildflowers, when I must not have been older than four. I'm really not sure what sort of flower, I've never been very good at naming flora—or fauna, for that matter. I only know they're flowers that you, my Love, found in your childhood and brought into our world because they had reminded you of me, of my eyes, and that meant they were safe to you.

It was where you started to build our land of dreams.

Over the years our world has grown, of course, but in the beginning it was just that little clearing of wildflowers, resting in the middle of an otherwise untouched forest. A safe and quiet world where we could be alone, peaceful.

A world that was *ours*, and no one else's.

And, before I get ahead to the more current timeline of the story, I'll take a moment to explain what lead you to create our safe haven in the woods. And how, before you had, nearly every night my dreams had been plagued by nightmares. Because, all my life I've been able to see more than most eyes can: and, one of the many ways I *do* is through the ability to see spirits.

All spirits.

When I was a child this made my mind a dark world without true shape. A darkness filled by so many other spirits that I lost sight of who, and what, *I* was. Because, these spirits come from all around the world, both living and no longer so—and, both when I'm awake as well as asleep—in such a quantity it's impossible to count. They always have: since, they know I can hear and listen to what they want, or need. But, back then especially, they rarely seem to realize I can't hear them at once, that it's impossible to help so many when I can't make out any single voice.

And, it used to be unbearable, until *you* learned how to keep the bad away. How to only let the good reach me—those who seek someone to guide them home, not those who only try to cause harm—and only when we're prepared to aid them. When I have you, my Knight, beside me and tethering me to the light.

Of course, the unkind still constantly await those little moments when you aren't there to buffer me, to *keep* them at bay. Taking advantage of those brief seconds, until you catch me and bring me solely back to you—your light. But, when I was a child, that was the sort who found me the most. They'd catch ahold of me, those spirits, and lock me in a world of endless halls: a maze where I could barely see anything around me, and what I *did* chance to see made me wish I hadn't.

I always started alone, running through the halls calling out to find someone I knew, to find *anyone*. A terrified little girl, lost and alone, until millions of shadows started to slowly pull away from the walls, out of doors that hadn't been visible before, and that I could never pass through once they were. Doors locked with a key that held the control of a world I could never quite hold on to.

As I passed by those doors, the shadows within would reach out to me. Clawing, to make me stop as I tried to run, yelling things that I couldn't understand. Crying at me for help, but never saying how I could when I begged them to tell me, in hopes they'd free me from the maze if I did: instead, they'd only try to drag me into the shadows, as I cried for the thing I feared the most… to be left alone.

Almost every night this happened, the same images spiraling through my mind. Me, running through those halls with tears blinding my sight, my legs and feet fighting my every step as if even they were an enemy. Screaming for help when no one could hear my voice, when usually no sound could even leave my lips.

I'd beg that world to let something, *anything*, wake me or say what I was supposed to do to end it. To stop the cold hands ripping my nightgown, cutting my skin as they tried to make me stop, to listen. Begging for something to stop them from hurting me, my spirit, to quiet those horrible *cries*.

All I wanted was to find the light again, to be free of that darkness…

And, every night this happened, *you* were my freedom. You'd somehow find me in the shadows—even when you had to fight through them, too—and then, you always knew the way through that maze, had the control of that world which I always lost.

You'd come for me within minutes if we both slept at the same time, which was rare since you went to bed before me, and tend to sleep less. I learned this, of course, when I realized the waking world operates in different time-zones, but didn't question it then. I knew my knight *would* come for me, and that was all I needed, because you always *do*: one second I'd be running through the halls screaming for help, and the next you'd come out of a door as I crossed it, saving me from the shadows as only you can. Catching one of my hands in yours, and guiding us out of there, without you ever needing to say a word—you'd simply meet my eyes, and I knew I was safe.

Because with you, my Love, I *am* always safe.

With you all the shadows faded from my sight, even when they were still present. I only saw you, and your eyes. I no longer felt the hands clawing at me, just your hand safe around mine as you lead us to the light: the secure, beautiful warmth of your skin sending all their cold away. As the protective weight of your impenetrable aura—the color of light butterscotch, of gentle amber—wrapped around mine, guarding us from everything around us.

Because, with you my whole world simply became *you*.

But, of course, sometimes it would be much later on in the night that you'd find me. Nights where, again as I learned later in life, you'd already woken for the day before I'd gone to sleep, and you couldn't get to me as easily. On those nights I'd run until I could no longer breathe, until all of me went numb to their hands scratching against my skin. Until I gave up hope, and curled in a ball against one of the walls, crying in silence, trying to ignore those screams.

Helpless… utterly helpless.

Yet, even when those nights found us, you still somehow *did* come for me. You said even awake you felt it, my call to you. Said you'd go back to near sleep, meditating before we knew what it was, just as you still do when similar moments happen.

Because you, my Love, *always* somehow come when I call for you.

You'd find a way to cut through the darkness, through the souls around us, and pull me out of fear to see you. And, on those nights you *would* say a word, because those nights I was so lost I didn't know you were there until you'd told me so. Your voice quieting all the screams around us. Just as I felt nothing except your arms around me, protecting me from the touch of anything else. Lifting me from that cold ground when I couldn't walk for myself, and carrying me out of there.

On those nights I'd only cry to you, unable to do anything else. Showing you every sad, hurt, desperate word and image the spirits had shown me—using telepathy before we knew what it was—and you somehow made everything alright, you always do.

Then, every night, as soon as we had left that darkness the entire world turned into a white light, and I'd be forced to wake up. Something that quite honestly had felt like the end of the world to me, as I was torn away from you. And, this happened until the day you found a way to create a whole world of our own outside of that darkness.

This was, as I said before, when I mustn't have been much older than four. I'm not the best at remembering age: what I see is always as clear in my mind as when it first happened, but I usually find I was younger than I felt. That night, instead of waking up as soon as we found the light, we stepped through it, and found those wildflowers.

It was the night I realized where our home really was.

And, I'd never seen a sight more beautiful. But, as lovely as they are, not because of the flowers themselves… but because of *you*, my Love—my home. As we stepped out of the brilliant light, our little hands tightly intwined from the horrible nightmare of before, my eyes were only on yours: how your usually sad eyes lit up with a pride, a happiness, I had never seen shining in your irises before. Because, you knew that *you* had made a safe haven where *nothing* could hurt us.

A haven only we could find.

After that night, the nightmares came far more rarely. Because, we finally had somewhere to go. Somewhere to envision as we fell asleep where we knew we could meet the other without fail or question. So, instead of stepping into darkness, when my eyes closed to my waking reality they opened again to that little sea of wildflowers.

You were always there before me, still always are. I'd often wonder if you'd waited all night in your reality for me to come there for the little while we had, but now I know you did. Because, when *you* had to leave, to wake up, I stayed waiting for you in case you may come back—because, sometimes, you did.

And, it was among those perfect wildflowers where we truly got to know the other as another human, not just a spirit who we loved entirely. I learned who you were, and how you were; what name you went by; about your home, family, and life. I learned you truly *are* a reality. That we aren't just the other's dream, but *true*. And, that's how we truly started to see each other in the waking world, too.

Just as true to our eyes as anyone else physically standing there.

Because, we *were*: thanks to that perfect sea of flowers, and how it gave us freedom to learn dreams aren't the limit to who we are when together, or what we're capable of when we're united, that there's far more—more than we could have imagined.

And, well, you and I never parted again from that day on, not fully.

So, only a few months after you made our clearing, you started to expand our world into the forest beyond. To shape the beautiful land where we could grow up together, even if we were far apart. As you said, "far closer than most who are side-by-side."

And, in those trees we used to play games, and be as free as children can be, racing one another to see who could make it the farthest before we would have to wake. As we always inevitably had to. It was a race that you'd always let me win, being a slow runner as I am, letting me think I really *did* win: and, doing just the same even after I caught on you were letting me.

We found an ease in this world that let us, quickly thereafter, learn how to stay in this spiritual land later, longer, gaining more conscious as ourselves. And, this allowed you to let the trees break away in our running to reveal the rolling hills beyond... here you'd let me run a little ways ahead, over a few of those hills, letting me think I had a lead before you easily caught up to me, and caught *me*. You'd always lift me from the ground as you did, just to make me laugh. Then, to my delight, you'd spin us in circles until you would usually send us rolling down one of those hills.

You'd make me laugh more than anyone else, and you still do.

This is where, after many months, I had stood when I first caught a glimpse of what my future would be. Of what *our* future would be. Where I stood, when I realized you hadn't just created a world from nothing, but from where you really were, in the *other* world. That every detail was derived from all the beautiful visions you saw every day in your waking life: from the true sights of *your* reality.

By then, I was likely five years old.

It had been too clear, too beautiful to be anything but true, and that was all the proof I needed. When you and I had been sitting atop one of those hills, talking about things that seemed important as a child but never was to anyone else, I had looked out over those beautiful rolling hills to see the lone tree sitting on top of a hill far away from us. A tree that looked like a big bonsai, to me: remember, I am admittedly not the best at naming things like that correctly.

But, the sight called me to its side, and I didn't fight it.

Standing up and running to where it was without any warning, or thought, slipping from your arms before you could think to stop me. Though, if we're totally honest, I'm pretty sure I did exactly what you hoped and knew I would, as I always do, so you didn't even *try* to stop me.

I came near enough to rest my hand against its bark, to feel its gentle heat against my palm. Before I rested my forehead against its side, and then turned to rest against one of my ears, to hear the heartbeat pulsing inside, the life few stopped to feel nature carrying. Because, that tree was far more than just a symbol to me: from the moment I saw it, I knew it was the beacon that would guide me to you.

The answer I've always searched for.

I kept my ear against its side for many heartbeats, with my eyes closed, listening as though it held the power to tell me everything that I needed to know. But, it spoke in a language I couldn't yet fully understand. Listening until the wind, gentle and kind, brushed across my face stronger than before, enough to push my long hair behind my shoulders—at the time, I'd been determined to let it grow to my ankles, to be quite like Rapunzel, but never did get it so—because, that wind held the answer for me. It made my eyes open to the land around us.

A world of green as far as the eye could see, unlike anything I'd seen before.

My voice was soft as that wind, so light no one else would ever be able to hear me, but you did. You *always* somehow do. "It's like a story."

I turned to rest my back against that tree, to meet your eyes. Those beautiful eyes, staring right back up at mine, that saw all of *me* and nothing else: understanding a girl who everyone else struggled to make sense of.

A wide grin crossed my face, at the sight of your own. The smile I only truly show you. A smile only you can create. "It's like a dream, isn't it? I mean, it *is*. You've told me it is. But, you know, something real and *like* a dream, but not really. Is this real? It is, isn't it? Has to be… *Feels* real."

You had fallen to sit under the tree as soon as we reached where it stood, picking absently at the grass as I listened to the Earth's secret words, watching me. And, when you spoke you only did so softly, with a voice that now isn't so soft but still quiet. A voice which carries an accent that rolls like thunder before a storm, one I didn't know the source of at the time: I only knew you spoke "funny," differently than anyone else in my life. And, well, in the best, most perfect way. You only said one word, but you never do use more than you have to, "Yeah."

"And, it's the most *beautiful* thing you've ever seen, isn't it?"

"S'alright." You shrugged, just one shoulder as you always do. "I guess."

"More than 'alright,' silly. Look. The green, the hills... *This*." I turned against the tree, hugging it before falling to sit beside you. As close as I possibly could. "Don't you see it, too?" One of my hands found yours to stop you from plucking at the grass. Drawing it into my own lap, and tracing your fingers. "It's ours... isn't it?"

Your eyes studied my face, every inch of it, for a long time. You did that often, still do, thinking through every word long before you say it, creating a silence most would probably find too long, but I never do. I always happily wait, watching those perfect eyes for the words you're going to say.

The eyes that say more than words can.

Your brows drew forward as they always do when deep in thought, as though you are considering the most profound thing known to mankind. And, usually... you really *are*. The smallest smile crossed your lips, whispering another single word. A perfect word, that was most definitely worth my wait. "Ours."

My smile somehow grew, spreading across my face in likely goofy proportions, a laugh leaving my lips. More of a giggle, really. A soft sound, and yet the happiest one can surely be capable of creating. I fell against you as I did, I frequently did and still do. My arms wrapping around you, hugging you as I never hug anyone else, my face buried against your chest. My ear pressed tight over your heart, again as I always did and typically also still do, to hear the steady sound that proves you're real.

That you're with me.

The thought of having somewhere that was just that, *ours*, where no one else could come and find, or bother us… someplace where I can be with you—without anyone or anything trying to take me away from you, or you from me—where nothing can come between us, that's the best thought in the world to me.

The greatest cause for happiness.

So, every time after then over the years of our life, when I mediate or look to see what our future will hold, I see the same thing: you and I, though much older than we were back then, sitting underneath that same perfect tree overlooking all those endless hills, one soul intwined in two beings.

Overlooking a world of freedom, surrounded by *love* and nothing else.

The dream guiding me to write this for you, my Love, began much as the world you created had… though, we're now just a wee bit older than five, aren't we?

We were laying among those flowers, watching the clouds slowly floating across the sky, lost in the world of one another. With my head resting over your perfect heart, listening to its steady, calm rhythm thumping against my ear as my fingertips absently traced your chest. With my other hand held in yours over my waist, your gentle thumb brushing over my knuckles, memorizing every last part of my hand.

How long we were there I don't know: time to us frequently becomes unimportant. Laying in a silence filled only by our soft breathing—because we don't ever *need* to use words, or anything but feeling, when our minds share thoughts—and by the wind as it gently rustled the leaves of the trees rising high up around our haven, surrounding and shielding us from the outside world.

We watched those clouds, our minds making stories to the images and shapes they created without really knowing we were. Our ideas and perspectives merging into one; our thoughts moving with the other's in an easy flow, never fighting the other's train of thought, never questioning where our minds took the tale we made, spiraling in one steady rhythm. Somehow, we've always thought so vastly differently than each other that we naturally find a balance between us that works: with the simplicity that always exists when something is *right*, and entirely connected.

Of truly being two as one.

That night, it had started with a cloud shaped as a ship, sailing across that smooth, endless blue sea of the sky. And, as that ship found its way home, at a dock on a shore far away from where it had started, my eyes finally chose to leave that sight to find the side of your beautiful face: honestly, the perfect sight of my home. And, even as you knew mine left it, your focus stayed set upon that sky, letting me study you with a freedom few would ever let another stare with.

A trust.

The only sign that would have given away you knew I was studying you, if I hadn't known before, was the tell-tale little twitch of your lips as you tried to fight a smile. One that was soon set free, when you quickly lost the battle. Letting those perfect lips rise ever so slightly on one side, as they always do, at first—whenever I get that side to rise enough to expose its canine, I feel like the most accomplished woman in the world; and, when I get *both* sides to rise in pure unhidden happiness, when the skin around those eyes crinkles in that true and absolutely magnificent smile... well, I feel like a Goddess who's capable of creating anything.

Because, your happiness is the most beautiful sight in my world.

My hand left where it rested over your chest to tuck your hair gently behind one of your ears, out of your eyes. Asking your gaze to come down from the sky, down to meet mine, as my fingertips slowly glided down the side of your face to let my thumb find your chin. Gently turning you towards me as my index finger feathered over your bottom lip, softly parting it from the other.

In a way that got your smile to quirk further over those lips.

One crossed my own at the sight, as I broke the silence surrounding our world: as I said what we usually do when we start to remember we have voices, "Hi."

"Hey." You spoke against the fingertip I still had over your lips. In a voice that was now far lower, far less timid than it had been in that memory I mentioned, truly rolling like thunder before a storm.

We almost always approach the situation about to occur this same way. We always have. Making your smile grow as mine did the same, exposing that canine for a flash of a second, before you kissed the tip of my finger and I let it glide down to your chin. Feathering over the coarse hair covering your skin, to where my thumb waited.

I tilted my face to kiss your shoulder, as high as I could reach where I was, and said those words we always choose to say aloud, even if we don't have to. Those words it's impossible to ever say enough. "I love you."

"Yeah?"

"Yeah." I lifted slightly away from you. Pulling myself up higher so my face was level with yours, with my body almost entirely on top of your own. Something I never would have been able to do, at least not easily, if you hadn't helped pull me there with the hand you held around my waist, knowing where I wanted to be.

Because, you wanted me there, too.

I kissed the tip of your nose—your perfect nose—quickly and just so. Getting that smile to quirk back higher, and those perfect eyes to sparkle like the sea beneath the sun. "But, you know, just a little bit."

"Good… 'Cause, *I*," Your hand, rough from callouses yet gentle as no other touch can surely be, found the side of my face to draw me nearer. Near enough for my nose to be right alongside yours: for us to only see our eyes as you kissed me, so long and sweetly. Keeping your lips against mine as you spoke, in the skilled way you have which may as well be kissing me still. Kissing endlessly. "Love *you*. But," you kissed me again, as only you can, "only a *wee* bit."

That laugh, the happiest I know how to make, left me.

And, you caught that sound. Your lips finding mine as soon as they parted, because you knew it'd come, letting your tongue easily find its way to my own the moment our lips met. Entwining smoothly, and passionately. Deeply, as you always do: giving me everything you are, and taking full possession of the mouth I so willingly give in return. Making my hand slip from the side of your face, and into the thick hair at the nape of your neck to hold you to me, to ask you to never leave.

To never stop.

You kissed me stronger when I asked, somehow you always can, turning your body from beneath mine to lay my back gently against the warm Earth: giving enough of your weight to feel all of you over all of me, but no more than that. Your hand gliding from my waist up to tenderly find my breasts, as you guided me down—as the other stayed where it was on the side of my face, keeping me there—taking full advantage of how all of me fits your hands perfectly.

Made for you, and for *you* alone.

A groan, which I felt through all of me, rumbled deep in your chest as your thumb pushed gently beneath my breast. Freeing it to the rest of your hand, and letting your skin find mine. Drawing a soft moan from my lips as you tenderly caressed me, as my back instinctively arched into your touch: because, I never want anything more than I always want you.

And, you groaned back. Your hips applying more pressure to mine, just enough to show how badly you needed all I wanted to give; how badly you wanted all of me. As that hand left my breast to skim its way slowly down my stomach, and to my hips—caressing and loving every inch between—gliding down to find one of my thighs. Letting your hand slowly start to edge the fabric of my skirt up higher, to see if I truly wanted to go further.

I pulled away from the kiss, just enough to meet your eyes. To leave no doubt of my response to your question, had there been any:

receiving a quick flash of your perfect smile before your lips found mine, skimming tenderly across my face as you slowly moved the fabric higher, enough to find the bare skin of my thigh. Letting that hand caress its way higher, too, as my own slid slowly down your chest, gliding across your stomach and yet lower to find the waistband of your jeans. Catching ahold of your belt, as the hand still within your hair drew your lips back to mine, easily pulling your belt loose and popping the button behind it free in one tug.

To set *you* free.

I kissed you, long and sweetly, caressing you with as much love as you caressed me back. Watching those glittering eyes fall closed as my touch drew another deep groan from your chest. The very masculine sort of groan that all my feminine senses... and muscles, instinctively react to. Making my hips rise to meet yours, my hand gliding onto your lower back, holding you to me.

Your lips trailed back across my face, slowly down my jawline, to my throat. And, my head tipped back, giving you access to anything you may want, as you kissed the sensitive hollow of my throat. As your soft tongue skimmed so very lightly across my skin, making my eyes fall closed—making my hand slip free of your hair to join the other, now splayed across your shoulder-blades, to hold you closer to me.

As your hand slipped from my hair to find my other thigh, your lips feathering from my collar-bone: catching the bow of my dress's tie between your teeth to easily free its ribbon, letting that kiss find the tender space just between my breasts as your nose nuzzled my dress out of the way.

Letting you love them both tenderly, in turn, as your hands slowly guided the fabric covering me fully to my waist. As my legs, equally slowly, wound around your body. Knowing where you needed me, and holding you to me just as and where you wanted. Offering you everything I am. As that slow, tender kiss feathered back over from my chest, up my throat, over my chin… planning to find my lips just as we would truly become one, as your beautiful eyes found mine. But, just before those lips *could* find mine, of course, that was when we learned the world had other plans.

Sometimes, things really *do* have poor timing.

Naturally, it wouldn't have been new for us to wake then, for our night to suddenly end right when we didn't want it to the most: that can sometimes happen when we rise with a passion the reality of dreams alone struggles to understand as a truly possible thing. But, usually, we can feel when the world is about to fall away and return us to the waking reality. Right then we felt no such thing. What we felt was something new, and entirely different: we knew this night still had a long ways before it ended.

That it had a strange, unexpected path set for us to follow.

You see, our world was then broken into by the solid sound of thunder cracking the Earth, making the world harshly jerk out from under us. Suddenly, and hard enough that it nearly made you lose your balance over me. You *would* have, if the suddenness of it hadn't made your instincts react faster than the Earth could quake, your body instantly bracing over mine, protective, in case it was something more than thunder. Sacrificing all of yourself to protect me, as you always instinctively do.

As I always do—and did then—for you, too.

Staying tense over me, unmoving, long after the sound vanished. Because, we both know what thunder means there, what usually happens if it breaks into our world, and it rarely means anything easy. Staying perfectly still, until the second crack of thunder: only then did you slowly pull your face away from where it had been tucked beside my own, to meet my eyes. Of course, we don't ever need words, but especially never in moments like that, our eyes saying every last thing for us. Because, we both knew that thunder was a warning of something we already had a feeling would happen.

And, we weren't afraid to show how much that terrified us.

You slowly shifted to sit beside me as that thunder faded, your head ever so slightly cocked as you tried to trace the sound backwards. Knowing that locating wherever it had struck would lead us to *why* it had. I didn't even try to do the same: my ears have never been as accurate as yours when it comes to things like that. I simply sat beside you, with you, my eyes staying set on yours.

Reading you, for the answers I wouldn't find on my own.

It didn't take you long to find it. By the time I fixed my skirts and tied my ribbon your head was no longer cocked, but I watched as your brows furrowed. Wordlessly, saying that you had a pretty good idea of where it had come from, and that the answer definitely worried you.

I was almost afraid to ask the question. If I wasn't such a curious person, perhaps I wouldn't have. My voice coming out barely above a whisper, "Where is it?"

You made that grunt: the low sound from far back in your throat, which oftentimes replaces words altogether, and can hold so many meanings. Nodding to your side, to indicate the direction we had to go, "'Tween here and the quarry, I'd say."

"The quarry…" I pushed myself up to stand, to put off knowing the answer to my next question for a little while longer. Shaking the stray flowers, and grass, that clung to my dress away before holding my hand down to you. Not necessarily to help you rise, but simply to touch some part of you. "Why there? Do you think."

"Can't say." Your hand found mine while you rose, not even pretending to use it for balance. Sliding the other around the side of my waist to draw me securely into your side, as close as I could be, once you had. Holding our joined hands at your calm heart as you kissed my forehead, right between my brows: reassuring as only you can ever truly be, for me. "Don't worry, that. M'sure it's fine."

You didn't give me any time to argue the likelihood of how un-fine it may really be. Honestly, the way that you're able to summon up any means of transportation you may want or need at any moment is something, like everything you do, that never ceases to amaze me. This night it was a horse who must be related to a Clydesdale in some way, with a long curling mane tending to hang in front of his dark eyes, and a tail mixed with whites and browns just like the rest of his painted coat. A horse who we've always called "Silence," for the reasons of how it snuck up on me now: before I knew what was happening, or that the horse was even there, you were already on its back and using the arm securely around me to pull me up in front of you; breaking into a run before my butt even landed.

The urgency—despite your words saying differently—declaring what I feared.

Making me instantly lean back, as soon as my butt *did* land, to tip my head onto your shoulder and look at you from a mostly upside down view. "Yet, you're sure we have to go?"

"M'sure. We have to find why, before…" You released a heavier breath, in place of your unspoken words. Those eyes—even seen upside down, as we were—telling me everything you were afraid to say aloud: that we had to go, before "why" found *us*.

A heavier breath left my lips, too, turning my gaze to the unmarked path ahead.

My body relaxing against yours despite what we knew was going to happen soon: they say Love shines brighter than any other light, don't they? Like a beacon, that can attract many forms of darkness to try and extinguish it. Even when love always wins, in the end… the darkness will always try to stop it from shining, won't it?

Well, this night, we knew it undoubtedly *would* try.

We rode until we reached the quarry, slowing where a barely marked dirt road—had we taken a road instead of going through the woods, we would've followed it—started to lead up to the mines. But, it was around the coming bend that the unbelievable sight of the stone rose above us, breaking out from behind the trees.

Seeming both near, yet miles away, at once.

It's hard to describe the sight well enough to convey how magnificent it is to really behold. But, it's a sight your eyes try to tell you isn't really there, when you know it is: a massive wall of slate reaching seemingly up to touch the sky, cut like mammoth steps made for giants to rise up to its highest ridge, up to find the sloping hills hidden somewhere on the other side.

I knew, from when you showed me this place in the past, that if you stood up on the higher plateaus, even just the second tier, you could easily see the village nestled in the valleys below. Appearing as a painting too perfect to be true. A quiet, perfect little town surrounded by magnificent mountains, where you could see every little boat in the water it bordered, the colorful dots moving slowly over the calm bay leading out to the sea. But, that was a view it would be impossible to find just then.

Up above the quarry's highest ridge we found where the lightning had struck, there was no way to deny it: up there, the world was raging with flames bright and blinding, pushing slowly over the land to find the woods waiting far beyond. Filling the vibrant sky—that was already merging from the orange and red hues of dawn into a more solid grey, as the clouds prepared for a nearing storm—with a hazy veil of smoke.

Making the air heavy, thicker than it should be.

Our eyes focused on the mountainside, however, rather than the fire. Focused on the reason the lightning had struck at all, what the Earth wanted us to find. Even from our distance we could see how, on the first plateau of that giant slate staircase, a thin crack was starting to splinter through the stone with fragile webs branching across the own, the worry in your eyes making it clear you didn't just mean at your side: there was a possibility that whatever would happen would tear me away from you, from that world; lost in a mess, alone, until you somehow found me again. Your head tipped down, resting your forehead against mine, your voice barely making a sound, "Stay *with* me."

I caught ahold of your belt, holding you to me, "I'm not going anywhere."

All my life, in both the waking reality and dreams, along with seeing spirits—as well as other "gifts" not yet named—I've had a gift of sight through touch. Whenever I touch anything, be it living or inanimate, I can see what they or it has experienced at the softest contact. I don't even have to touch, or be touched, with my hands for this to happen: if any part of me makes contact with something, my mind will be flooded with their feelings; as well as the images of either their past, be it their current life or another, their present with whatever they're thinking and seeing in that moment, or the possibilities of their future.

I don't have any control over what, or how, but I'm always shown something. It's a part of me that without fail leaves me feeling overwhelmed, intrusive in ways I can't rightly describe. And, there's no way to stop it from happening except to avoid contact as much as I can, to only touch what I have to: except animals or books, both of which are always calm and comforting, you're the only being who it entire wall: warning that it could fall, or crack open further, at any moment it chose.

"They aren't here." Your voice, lower than it usually is and barely audible, made a shiver run down my spine as your hot breath hit the back of my throat. Making me far too aware of how utterly empty the world around us was. Usually, in places like this, anyone can see the faint figures of light who watch over our world, but not then. Even I, who can see all spirits even *when* they hide, saw nothing.

It was only us.

You dismounted before that shiver had time to fully run down my spine: your boots landing with a solid *thump* on the Earth, seeming far louder than it should have been thanks to the worrying quiet around us. A sound that ended my shiver with a gasp as your hands found my waist, to lift me down in front of you.

"Stay at my side." Your eyes, swirling with a torrent of emotion, narrowed on mine. Saying far more than words ever could, "If anything touches you, say. Hear me?"

I nodded, openly too concerned to speak.

We both knew—no matter how dumb it seemed to walk right to the problem, since it's surely the number one cause of disaster in a horror movie—we had to investigate closer, otherwise we wouldn't be able to find the root of the problem at hand, and be able to fix it before it got worse. But, we also knew one of us would be significantly more effected by the possible reasons than the other… that, even if I were to wait by the horse as you went to look alone, said issues would inevitably swarm to where I was: we knew we didn't have a choice.

"Stay with me." You came closer, your chest pressing against my feels *right* to touch—who I *want* to feel and see all of, but you definitely already know that.

And, touching that wall of slate, was the first time I felt *nothing*.

My fingertips glided across the smooth, cold stone slowly as we walked towards the crack. My other hand held securely in yours as you guided us to where we needed to be, leading me blindly with my eyes closed, waiting for any part of it to speak to me. But, there was nothing, not even a whisper of the history we knew was cradled within: the memories of a hurt young man who had once walked this part of the world feeling as though he were slowly having his life stolen away, with no power to stop it. Just as the mountains surely feel when being mined.

Even as my fingertips bumped delicately over the fine lines of webbing, those new scars showing us the Earth's pain, I didn't feel it: the secret pulse of past emotions that once had been safely locked within these walls, was gone.

All I felt was cold stone: it was the other hand that saw *everything*.

"You... you opened it, didn't you?" My voice didn't carry true sound, but you heard me. Even if no one else can, you always do. My shaking hand gripping yours desperately, so tightly it surely must have hurt you, as my feet forgot how to walk further. Because, what I'd feared from the moment you said where we had to go stood right before us, no longer possible to deny. My eyes lifted to find yours, knowing you had been studying me the entire time, waiting for me to ask. "What happened?"

The slightest smile quirked over your lips, "You."

"*Me?*" I lifted a brow, "Whatever did *I* do? To make you... do that?"

"What haven't you done?" Your hand tightened around mine—as warm and safe as mine felt cold and afraid—speaking just as softly, if not even more so, as I had. But, of course, we *both* knew exactly what: your eyes always do tell me everything, even when your mind tries to hide the words. When your lips can't speak them, "But, you already know, yeah?"

"You know I do."

"Even... why?"

"Even everything." I came closer to you when your beautiful eyes suddenly turned glassy, with the very fear that had once been trapped behind that wall of stone. My arms wrapping protectively, tightly, around your waist: catching you, as you let your weight fall onto me, needing to hold me just as much as I needed to hold you. As you tucked your head securely alongside mine. "I know, and it's okay, my Love. I'm here. *With* you. Nothing will ever change that... you *know* that."

Truly, my Love, nothing will *ever* keep us apart.

That's why we didn't even react when we felt the fall of loose stones starting to rain down from above, the ground starting to quake softly beneath us. I only lifted a hand higher up your back to protect the back of your neck from the stones, as you did the same for me. Neither of us trying to leave, knowing better than to fight it: we heard the rumble of thunder singing through the air, and knew it wasn't the sort a storm could cause, but the sound of the world opening for a purpose no one could alter.

Not even us.

We felt the surge of dust burst from the second ridge with a heavier falling of stone, and then the ground beneath us vanished into open air. Plummeting us into darkness: a world for the spirits who hide from, and protect, what lies above.

But, we knew we'd be alright... together.

After a weightless fall which felt both impossibly long and oddly short at the same time, we were harshly reacquainted with that incredibly hard stone when I landed flat on my back, with you chest down on top of me: my head saved from cracking against the stone along with my body by your hand, which suffered that fate instead. Landing with such a force that the wind was knocked entirely from our lungs.

Yet, somehow, despite the lack of air you immediately tried to rise onto your hands and knees—suddenly stopping at just the height of your elbows, which didn't help my imagination in any way, shape, or form.

Your voice sounding blunted, shallow: the hot air of your breaths, unusually fast and heavy, pounding against my face as you tried to see me through the dense darkness. "Y'alright?"

A groan left me, in an attempt to say I *was* alright while trying to regain a breath to speak. One of my hands sliding from around your waist to find your chest, to feel your heart racing against my palm: I was able to say one word, "You?"

"S'long as you're in one piece, m'fine." Just in case I wasn't, the hand not cradling my head started an exploration, making sure no part of me was broken or hurt. At least every part of me you could reach, that is. "Your back?"

"M'okay, just…" I was interrupted by a laugh leaving my lips, your hand finding an incredibly ticklish part of my side, at the smallest part of my waist—though, to be fair, *all* of me is ticklish. It was something you did on purpose, I knew, fully distracting me from our predicament. "Stop that."

You didn't hide the smile in your voice, "Didn't break any ribs, then?"

"*No.*" I laughed again, because you *did* it again, getting you back by doing just the same to you. A wide grin crossing my face at the soft sound of your laugh: that silent, heavier release of breath. "Did *you*?"

"No." You kissed the tip of my nose, "You kindly broke the fall for me."

"And, *you* saved me from breaking my noggin." I kissed you blindly back, finding your cheek: your head was turned, your eyes obviously trying to see around us. Trying to figure out how to get us out of the situation, now that you were sure we were both okay. "Do you have any idea where we are?"

"Sure…" Your hand left my waist to rest on the stone beside my ribs. Bracing your weight as you tried to rise a bit higher, testing the space around us. I tried to ignore the sound of trickling stones in response, but didn't miss your whispered, "Shit."

"We're in shit, are we?" I tried to ignore the true meaning, "Sounds lovely."

"Oh, yeah." You laughed, this time with light sound, too. In a way that had a way of easing at least a bit of my rising anxiety. "One of my favorite places to go."

"And, by 'go,' I hope you mean leave."

"Yeah... soon as possible, preferably."

"You need light, then?" That grunt, a very protective one, was your quick response. But, my hands found either side of your face before you could voice the words in that grunt, turning you back towards me. "Shush. It won't take much, I'll be fine."

I refused to give a chance for you to argue, my blind eyes falling closed as I felt my aura grow out around me. Wrapping around *you*. Forming a safe sort of bubble around us, as the world lit up with my faint white light—one I never would have found, if not for you, long ago. It lit up the space only enough to see what was directly around us, but that was plenty for my breath to freeze in claustrophobic terror. When blind, I had only been aware of *you* tightly around me, trying my best to ignore how the walls of the space touched your shoulders, how it was too low to rise higher than your elbows because that was where your back met its curved ceiling. But, *now*, there wasn't a way to ease the facts so blatantly in sight: we were trapped in a coffin-like world, buried under loose stones which crumbled in around us at the slightest contact.

It was a good thing my light was helpful... since I otherwise wouldn't be.

"Hey." Your hand, still cradling my head, turned my eyes back to yours, away from the nearness of those walls around you. The calm, and safety in those eyes reminding breath how to return to my lungs.

Unlike me, only the briefest flash of panic had come over you at the sight of our world, vanishing just as quickly as it came with the power you always have that can turn the feeling into adrenaline on a dime if you see *my* fear. "Hold onto me, my light. Try and keep off the ground. Yeah?"

All I could manage was a nod, my returned breaths moving much too fast to allow for words. Wrapping my arms around you carefully, probably much slower than you wanted me to, avoiding touching the walls or ceiling at all costs. But, you didn't say a word, didn't rush me: you never do. I did the same with my legs only once my arms were locked around you, my knees hooking over yours when your hand left my neck to find my thigh, asking me to do just that.

My voice was barely a whisper, spoken right by your ear, "I can help you."

"S'alright." Your hand found my side, asking me to lift my body off the ground: you wanted to avoid scraping my back against the stone when you'd do what you had to, even if it would make it harder on yourself in the process. I didn't protest, I knew better than to try, using all of my strength to cling to you… like a monkey. "There's a way out. Just keep holding onto me, alright?"

I nodded, burying my face beside yours to keep my eyes from seeing. Only aware of the feeling of you, as you somehow started to crawl towards whatever exit you saw. Slowly, with the weight of us both, and carefully in an attempt not to touch anything, using mostly only your elbows.

You spoke between strained breaths, "You can keep the light without hurting, yeah?"

"Yeah." We were both all too aware of the fast pulse at the center of my forehead. The warning of our limited time, as its steady beat counted down the minutes we had left before I wouldn't have enough energy left for the light. A warning that made my voice even softer than it usually was, afraid. "Don't know how long, but yeah."

"S'alright." You kissed my shoulder, the only part of me you could reach with how tightly my arm was wrapped around your neck: the other hooked under your shoulder, my hands clinging to each other, and your shirt, somewhere on your back. "Let it go when you have to, we'll find the way. S'long as y'stay with me."

"I promise," I clung to you tighter, my light growing brighter despite the fear of it fading sooner: sometimes, I can't control that. "I'm not going anywhere."

After a long and careful time, you managed to crawl out of the tight space and into the wider tunnel beyond. A tunnel more similar to a narrow hallway, its walls formed out of rough edged stone, slate, instead of falling dirt: a tunnel that we simply laid in, catching our breath, after you rolled off of your elbows and onto your back, with me laying over you, your arms hugging me tight against you.

We stayed just so for a decent sized moment, simply breathing.

"You," A soft, breathless laugh left me, blowing my hair—wet from the sweat of your chest, but you know I never mind that—out from its mussed place over my face. I was out of breath just by holding onto you, and yet your breaths were already back under control, despite the effort you had undergone a moment before. "You really do amaze me… you better know that."

"Likewise." You grunted, a sound that was a smile all of its own, "And, don't try to say you did nothing."

"Hm," I kissed your chest, right over your pounding heart, "Even if I didn't?"

"You're here, aren't you?" One of your hands left my back to find the back of my throat, holding me to your heart. Its heavy weight making my eyes fall closed, safe as only you let me feel. "Would have no desire to leave, if you weren't. Y'know that… probably too well, yeah?"

I did know, and yes, *far* too well: you wouldn't have thought your own life, alone, was worth saving. A heavy breath left my lips, kissing you again, "I *am* here."

"Yeah, you are." You made that grunt, the smile, "Amazing me all the while."

"Mm…" My eyes peeked through my remaining mussed hair to see the way ahead. My light slightly expanding around us in an attempt to see the subtle movement I *felt* shifting in the darkness there: those figures who start out just shy of appearing human, merely shadows, and tend to only show their true faces to me… who usually only try to *approach* me. "Does that mean you're okay to keep going?"

Another grunt, "No longer alone, then. Are we?"

"Less so by the moment."

"Then, yeah." Your arms loosened in that tight hug, your hand leaving my neck to find my lower back, patting me just the once.

Telling me you weren't just *okay* to keep going, but rather eager to. I slid off of you, onto my knees, the moment you asked it. Watching as you rolled yourself over to your chest, pushing yourself up to your knees, then your feet: I didn't miss the fatigued wobble you tried to hide as you stood. Lifting my brow when your eyes met mine, holding a hand down for mine, "M'fine."

"Uh-huh." I took that offered hand, accepting the aid, as you drew me up to your side. Bumping my arm gently against yours to get your lips to quirk up into a smile, keeping that hand securely in mine. "Just don't pass out, alright? That's my job."

"Nah, don't worry, that." Your smile lifted to expose that canine, bumping me back, before you started to lead down the hall. But, your eyes stayed on mine, of course, always making sure I'm alright. "Much more likely to swoon, aren't I?"

A laugh left me—at a memory only we'll ever know, I promise you—successfully making me forget about the shadows, "You're such a sweet dork... you know that?"

"Undoubtedly." You squeezed my hand, as those beautiful eyes softly crinkled with your perfect smile: making *me* smile, as nothing else can. "Your dork, my light."

"And," I drew our entwined hands up to my lips, "My Everything."

We continued down the winding tunnels silently, lost in the quiet sort of trance that comes over a mind when it's focused on one task.

When all you can hear are footsteps and breaths: when all you can do is keep walking until you reach a way out, no matter how far it has a possibility of being.

When you don't want to think how far that may be.

You had to walk severely hunched through the tunnels, your shoulders still brushing either side. Blocking all sight of what was ahead with your body, unless I chose to see through your eyes. Your long, quick strides stable despite all the loose stones shifting over the tunnel's deceptively steep slope, leading down further into the Earth. Despite my hand between your shoulder-blades, using you to keep *my* balance as I repeatedly lost it. Leading down the seemingly endless tunnel steadily, determined, looking for any variation in the path that may say if we were getting close to an end.

And, it appeared after what felt like an eternity of walking, as we turned down one of the many identical bends leading yet deeper: the faintest shift of stray light in the distance. A single flame, burning like a beacon in the darkness, silently calling us to follow with a promise that the way would soon become illuminated by torches, and—the only part that truly mattered to you—that my light could soon slightly ease.

As it did, the moment we stepped into the firelight. Letting us continue through the winding tunnel slowly, without the fear of our light fading. Slowly, and carefully since we knew we truly were no longer alone, our eyes jumping to any shift of the flames in case the shadows may be alive. But, never once glancing down the dozens more unlit paths that split off along its walls: the tunnels we knew eventually lead to the hallways that had once nightly plagued us.

We only followed the fire… cautiously.

It lead us to a narrow set of stone stairs, so narrow that you had to walk sideways to avoid scraping its rough walls. And, so eerie that I once again pushed my aura brighter around us, letting my view of the world open up a bit more as you took the first step down those stairs. Doing so despite the strain it put back on my forehead, or how you tried to stop me when you knew it'd very quickly deplete what was left of my energy. Letting my senses reach the strange out-of-body experience where we can see further than eyes can, just in case there was life we couldn't see.

Or, I should say, in case there was a more *solid* shadow below.

You paused at the base of that twisting staircase, seeing from my thoughts instead of your eyes what was waiting beyond. And, that was when we saw the single dancing light far down the next stretch of tunnel—watching without eyes, just my feeling—as it broke slowly away from the rest. Watching, as that bobbing light began to turn into a human-shaped shadow walking our way.

Staying as a dark, solid mass even as it came closer.

You kept your back against the inner-stairwell, out of sight, waiting for it to come to us instead of approaching it. Your hand slipping out of mine, telling me to stay back, as the other slowly found the back of your waistband, taking your knife from beneath your shirt, just in case. Listening as its slow, calm steps drew closer, crunching softly over the loose stones.

All I could do was stand still, a couple steps above, not even breathing.

Waiting, until they stepped into the light of the stairwell. Letting *my* light reveal the spirit hidden inside. It was a "face" you didn't see at all, only the shape of where it should be, the vague outline; but I saw the bright flickering flame of what that face *really* was, casting shadows of sharp angles, of skin vibrantly glowing with its own fire... of eyes shining gold, holding far more knowing than a human eye can. The face of many who live in the shadows of the Earth, a *part* of every piece of Earth.

Most, I suppose, call them one of the faeries.

Of course it's safe to say I've seen a great many spirits in my life, of every kind and variety, and am used to how they're typically compelled to use my energy to power theirs, to show themselves. But, there are still rare times when the sight's unexpected, and the power they need is more than I'd prepared for them to require.

And, both have the power to take all breath away.

I heard the startled gasp leave me. Felt your aura instantly snap around mine to stop the other from taking more than they had to, from me, pushing the other back. Felt the wave of your protective energy envelop me, catching me. But, not before I felt myself tipping forward, as my knees lost all semblance of support. Falling, weightlessly and once again blindly, right into your waiting chest.

Only vaguely aware that my ankle rolled sideways on the step, as I did.

"We were waiting for you." The spirit's voice was neither male or female. Speaking as my eyes heavily blinked open and met theirs: rather easily, thanks to how my head was resting on your shoulder, in that direction. Letting a bright smile, that you could see, too, stretch across their otherwise featureless face, despite the blade held beneath their chin—by your hand, the one not holding all of me. "If we may?"

I lifted a far too heavy hand up to rest on your extended arm's elbow. Lowering the blade away from the shadow, as my equally heavy head lifted from your shoulder to find your eyes. Speaking softly, "It's okay… they only want to talk, I'll be fine."

"Yeah. S'long as they're quick about it." You returned the blade back to where it'd come from, lifting me up to be cradled in your arms before I could protest. Not that I would have, you knew: even when I could have, in theory, managed to walk at a likely slow pace, I'd never say "no" to being carried by you. It's one of my favorite things, after all. You nodded to the spirit, "Go on."

"Of course." They lifted a hand, one not holding a lantern, to wave vaguely toward the next hall. Starting to lead before even asking, "If you wouldn't mind following?"

You did, with a grumble intended only for my ears, "Don't think we've much a choice."

"No. It won't take but a moment, to save the world or destroy it." The spirit glanced back: right into your eyes, intensely, in a way that left little to be questioned. In a way that made you waver a step, holding me tighter to you. Making my arm, resting over your shoulders, tighten around you, too. "You will understand, soon."

You grunted, "Think I already do."

I'll pause here a moment to tell the first memory I had been given of your childhood, one that must have happened shortly—by your age

—around the first night in our little field of wildflowers. I've never known for certain rather it happened in your dreams, or waking reality, because I've never directly asked *where* it came from.

But, both possibilities are held the same for us, I suppose.

It was one of many memories you hadn't necessarily meant to share, and I've rarely mentioned afterward—I hope you don't mind my mentioning it here—since I know its effect on you: not because of *this* memory itself, but the many that followed. Because, it had taken place as your entire world started to fall apart.

I had been shown the vision when I least expected it. When I'd been in the shower, innocently singing one second, then on my knees seeing images that didn't belong to my mind in the next… it was when we started to break through the "static."

You'll likely be the only one who'll know what I mean by that.

"There you are." A woman's soft voice had been the sound to make my eyes open to the memory. The voice of your mother, out of breath from running to find you after you had strayed from the other kids and families in a park: this was the first time I saw the beautiful figure who so strongly resembles you.

You'd been kneeling alongside a quiet road just outside that park, admiring a small batch of those flowers, happiness shining in your rarely vulnerable eyes. You studied them as if they were the most important thing in existence, because to you they had been, lost entirely in your own world.

That world where you could exist untouched, alone.

She stopped at your side, watching as you reached one of your small hands out to catch ahold of the stems, pulling the flowers from the Earth gently, kindly. Careful as you always are. Only kneeling down beside you as you picked the stray weeds out of your small bouquet, your brows drawn forward in concentration as you made them all just so: *nothing* in the world existed to you beyond those wildflowers.

You hadn't even realized she was there. Instinctively jumping away from her touch as her hand softly landed on the top of your head; instinctively hiding the vulnerability in your eyes when they snapped up to hers, as soon as you left that private world, protecting yourself in a way that a child shouldn't know how to.

But, a way *you* were already starting to learn.

"Your da's growing impatient... Thinks you've gone and lost your mind, for a silly flower." A small smile crossed her lips, slowly rising back up to her full height—right around the same height as me, I believe. Her hands smoothing her somehow spotless white dress, that fell down to her knees, before she held a hand down to you. But, you rose on your own, already as timid of human contact then as you still are now.

We've always had that in common, for entirely different reasons.

She let it fall slowly back down to her side as her gentle smile forcibly grew, trying to feign lightness even when she was breaking apart inside. Just as any mother would, if they stood where she had: knowing *why* her child feared touch. "Between us, I think it's a *good* thing losing your mind to something silly. But, people like your da... they aren't kind to those who think differently, who see the *world* differently. You just ignore it, when he calls you things, alright?"

You only nodded, your eyes dropping back down to that bouquet.

"Those *are* lovely. Are they for me?" She took a step away, toward the way she had come from. You automatically went with her, your eyes cast down, shaking your head only once, but she already knew. "For your angel, then? The one in the stars."

You nodded, almost imperceptibly, as she gently tucked a stray strand of your hair behind an ear. Leaning away, and looking up at her as she did to give a falsely irritated glare. One that almost gave away how you hadn't completely minded. But, she didn't notice—I barely had—her eyes falling onto the now revealed half of your face, whose smooth skin was reddened and swollen.

From the hand of one who was supposed to *protect* you.

"I'm sorry my eyes are too blind to see her, too." She dropped her hand back down to her side, her soft smile returning even when her eyes showed the same heartbreak, the same helplessness, that I felt at the sight. "Maybe, my little romantic, when your da's out tonight you can tell me about her."

She reached out to muss your already messy hair. And, this time, you looked up at her with a small smile across your lips, letting her do so. "Maybe, then I'll see your kind angel, too. Would you tell me?"

"I can?" Your voice came out softly, cracking on the vowels.

Her smile widened the rest of the way, a light sparkle entering her eyes, "You can *always* tell me, baby."

Your gaze dropped back down to the flowers, happiness slowly returning to your eyes, as she shifted a slight step closer. Bumping into your side to draw your attention back up to hers, to meet your happy eyes while they still were. And, this time, you gently bumped her back, a smile crossing your face.

She had given you a sign that you weren't as insane as the world claimed you were, that day. And, I believe, that added another layer of safety around those flowers: they were no longer just a reminder of my eyes, but a sign of hope. Because, with them in your hands, someone had *listened*.

But, I suppose, you already know that...

Around the bend, the winding tunnels had been smoothed and leveled into one of the hallways that didn't belong underground. Its floors and walls shining in dark gray marble, so polished we could clearly see our reflection in the stone as we passed by.

The spirit lead halfway down that long hallway. To where the stone, on either side, had been covered by a giant canvas. One that had to span twenty feet across, but likely more—I've also never been great at gauging distance. It lined the halls like wallpaper: forming an amazingly detailed map of where everything in our vast world was, both above the surface and below.

What we needed, that simple disguise only you could truly understand, was right in the center of that canvas. On a very *specific* part of the map. You stopped just before the small, perfect bouquet of flowers, tied with a white ribbon. Waiting there, right at your eye level. You slowly lowered me down to, at least somewhat, stand on my own. Holding me to your chest as it heaved with breath you couldn't quite find, just as mine was, keeping me supported by your arm.

You took it carefully off the canvas the moment a hand was free. That hand, as well as all of you, visibly shaking. Because, you knew what that touch would do, and there was no way to be prepared for it, no matter how much you expected it: you couldn't stop the flood of images that tore through our mind.

Memories you desperately try to keep in the dark, and for that reason I won't get into any detail about them here. I'll just say, the images traveled quickly along every twist of the road that lead you to where you are, the road that made *you*, my Love.

Every flash showing how, what, and why you survived... for us.

"This land will always be *yours*." The spirit spoke as you closed your hand around those stems, letting the flowers become what they really had been: a heart-shaped key, which perfectly fit within your palm, and yours alone. "*You* hold this world, its heart, in your hands... *they* will try to steal it from you, and *you* must *protect* it."

You didn't say a word, we didn't have to.

"When *we* are gone, *they* will be free. And *you*, alone, will stand between the light and the dark." The spirit resumed leading further down the hall as they continued to speak, knowing we'd follow. As you did: before I realized they were walking again, I was already in your arms. "When they try to *break* your key, to leave you blind in the darkness, trust the hand that holds it: trust the mind that can see *beyond* the sun. And, you'll then *catch* the shadows. You understand?"

You grunted, affirming you did.

"Know, they will try to stop you by tearing out the *roots* and destroying our tree... but, the roots will yet grow beneath the sun, when the night is banished. When the key unlocks the *day*." The spirit stopped where the hallway turned back into the tunnels, already vanishing before the last word was said: knowing you wouldn't pause or look back. Only I did, because a part of me feared what it'd meant by one of those words. "You have to free the *light* from the one who can see *below* the soil, my friend. Only then will the light be free, and only when the *light* is free, can *you* unlock the door. I know you understand."

It was after the last word that the ground began to violently shake with a trembling roar. That we were hit by a surge of heavy pressure, that made even you stumble: a hot rush of power that made the walls instantly crack—the tunnels beginning to cave in as the world started to break apart.

So, after the last word... you started to run.

By the magic and sometimes impossible sciences of that reality, where it had taken us what felt like hours to find our way down to that canvas, it took you seconds to find the way out. At the end of the hall, after the spirit vanished, there rose another twisting staircase leading upward. And, I'm not sure if it *was* an incredibly short staircase, or if it just seemed to be, but we flew up without seeming to touch the steps: as you took it at *least* two stairs at a time in each stride.

Then, at the top of that staircase, we found the blinding world outside.

Your feet touching the stone of the quarry just as a loud concussion rang out at the opening you'd just cleared, and the ground beneath us suddenly pulled out from under you. Thankfully, you were able to fall into a roll when you felt your boot slip, landing on your back instead of your face. But, lost your grasp on me as your breath was again thrown from your lungs—not only from the fall itself, but the terrible pain I felt pierce your side—sending me rolling until my stomach collided with a tree's trunk, stopping with my back facing both you and the quarry.

I heard the thundering crack as the mine caved in; felt the hot rush of air that came along with it, strong enough that you slid over to join me at that tree, pushing a heavy force of dry rock-dust over us. Heard the wall start to creak, as the Earth continued to quake, moaning in a warning to all below. Heard, as that wall of stone began to fall: as the cliff that had once stood tall, and strong, fell down in a heavy rain of stone, sliding down from the highest ridge in an avalanche of destruction.

But, I saw nothing: you had me under you as soon as you slid against me, as soon as the wall started to fall. Covering *all* of me, but only protecting *your* head with your arms. Pinning me so tightly to the ground that I couldn't move to protect you, leaving the rest of you exposed to be pelted by shards of falling stone.

Until, a heavy sheet of rock landed on top of us.

It lasted no more than five seconds, but that's all it took to destroy the once majestic quarry, and flatten the woods around it. To bury us in stone, several feet deep, with its immense weight pressing us tight against the cracked Earth: we only had the pocket of air you'd made with your arms around our faces to breathe; your entire body crushed over mine, making it near impossible for you *to* breathe. But, we were both unnaturally calm, waiting to make sure the world stopped shifting before you started to move.

I, myself, was far too pinned to move a muscle.

But, somehow, you managed to unwind your arms from around your head, planting your forearms on the ground around *my* head. Using all your strength to shove us free of the heavy stone, with your back: releasing what little breath you had in one yell, as you strained to find freedom. Freeing your shoulders and head first, in a way that also freed my arms, too, from where they'd been trapped under your chest. Letting me use what little strength I had to push against that heavy sheet of stone with you: planting my hands just beside your ribs to lift it from your hips; and then, as far off your back as I could solely manage, once my knees were free to do the same.

It was barely enough room for you to yank your legs free, and crawl out of the slate prison, but thankfully that was my only purpose. By the time my strength was giving out, you were free to lift that stone with your arms, rather than your back, letting me crawl free, too: letting us both flop on top of those stones, our chests heaving; laying side by side facing one another, studying one another to see how we were.

I was still relatively untouched, thanks to you, only covered in a very light amount of dust and sweat. But, all of you—sparking a bright flood of worry through me—was either stained red from blood, from where the stones had cut you, or dusted gray from the slate and dirt, covered in a very heavy layer of sweat.

One of my hands rose to clumsily brush slick hair out from your face, as your eyes closed to avoid the glare of the sun. Flattening my hand over your too-hot forehead: to feel it throbbing under my palm with every beat of your too-fast heart, just as I saw it quivering in your every limb. Feeling how, to you, everything seemed incredibly hot, where to me it seemed fairly cold.

Which meant there was something undoubtedly *wrong*.

My energy wrapped around you, trying to see what, how and where you were hurt. But, you—stubborn as you are—somehow blocked my sight, refusing to show me. In a way that concerned me even more: it could only mean something was *very* wrong. I pulled myself closer to you, my voice quiet and dry, "Where?"

"M'fine." Your voice was equally dry, and rough, "You?"

"I'm perfectly fine, thanks to you. But, you already know that." I leaned over you, letting the hand not on your forehead find your too-fast heart. Closing my eyes to feel *inside* of you, but still you stubbornly fought me, only letting me see the minor things wrong. My voice became much more breathy, "You know, it wouldn't hurt you to take a moment to consider your own well being from time to time, my crazy man."

You made that grunt, a laughing one, "Sure… if you do the same."

"Not a chance." My hand slid from your heart down to your side, the one further away from me—my eyes snapping open with a gasp, when I felt the growing wetness across your shirt, and the undeniable shard of stone protruding from your skin. Just as I'd assumed, the problem was the answer to the sharp pain I'd felt when we fell out of the quarry, that you so immediately hid from me, knowing what I'd try to do. "Roll to this side. Let me see, you stubborn fool."

"Not now." You suddenly sat upright—those words truly a grunt

—nearly knocking your forehead against mine, as your hand found mine to take it away from your side and up to your lips. Kissing me as if there wasn't a problem: but you couldn't hide the wince that crossed your face. Your eyes begged me to ignore it, nonetheless, making mine narrow on yours, "You heard what it said, we can't stay here."

"It will only take a second."

"Yeah... but, w'both know it'll take more than *time*, don't we?" You winked, at my still narrowed eyes, as your free hand reached behind me to catch ahold of something: I hadn't heard the big horse come up behind us, but this time I wasn't surprised. You'd caught ahold of its bridle, letting him help you—as well as my arm carefully around your waist—to your feet. Slinging one of your heavy arms around his throat, and the other over my shoulders, to take your weight as you regained equilibrium.

Letting your head rest heavily on top of mine as you swayed, as our eyes only then lifted up to see the damage around us. A sight that made you pat the horse, just once, "Good horse... finding us in this."

My voice was even more breathy than before, "*Very* good."

The avalanche had poured from the cliff in a merciless wave. Destroying everything except for one thing: the tree, that'd held its ground just long enough to protect us, its trunk bent rather than snapped like the rest, barely peeking out of the rubble where we had been. A shield saving us from becoming a true part of that rubble, too. If not for that tree, we would have been truly trapped, if not flattened like the forest in that sea of stone. Where now, only jutting shards of wood defiantly spiking out from breaks in the rocks marked what it could have been—the quarry now just a steep slope of loose, and jagged stone: a mountain of rubble instead of a majestic image of strength defying gravity, as it had been before.

"Good thing," you drew me tighter to your side, "I've an angel guarding me."

I grunted, as you do, "Not doing a very good job, is she?"

"Doing a'pretty amazing job, considering she's a lunatic to guard." You once again caught ahold of its bridle, that smirk of yours quirking higher as a soft laugh left me. Starting to walk us carefully, at the horse's side, through the precarious slope of loose stone stretching at least a mile into the distance. "All this for a'flower… if that doesn't showcase insanity, dunno what does."

"True…" I gently bumped against you, "But, I do so love that about you."

"Yeah." You stretched your hurt side to ease the pain splitting from your hip up to your chest. Not complaining when I gave more of my energy to you, as you pressed your arm—the one not on my shoulders—against it. Trying to stop the bleeding in my way, just as you did. "'Cause, you're the one who *drives* m'mad."

"Mhm. And, I'm not sorry."

"Good," You said the word in a grunt, swinging somehow easily up onto the horse's back once we made it to a relatively flat part: a back covered by a saddle, I should say, with satchels slung over the horse's hips to hold all we may need. "Don't want it any other way, my Life."

That was when it *truly* started, when the bad things found us.

I was just about to take your extended hand, to join you on the horse, when I felt it. The undeniable wave as something changed, a shift of a horrible second that moved in slow-motion minutes. It began with the stronger gust of air, that *only* hit me. A blast of cold: the sort that raises the fine hairs on your arms... that foretells a really bad storm.

That warns you of darkness.

Air, that lifted my eyes to the madly swaying treetops, at the end of the stone sea, just as you reached that hand down for me. Air, that made my breaths freeze, solid in my lungs, made my body forget to move, as though I'd been turned to ice. I heard you say my name, yelling for me, but my ears heard as if you were suddenly miles away; I felt your fingertips graze across my arm, so safe and warm against my icy skin, trying to catch ahold of me... but then I heard the screams, silencing all other sound in the world. Then, I saw the thick black smoke burst out from those trees, as a true wave of that cold, painfully numbing air slammed into all of me—pulling me into a whirlwind, of smoke suffocating me, of shadows clawing at me, of darkness eating me.

Yet, even as my body lacked the ability to react, to even scream, and I felt myself suddenly getting stolen away... I wasn't afraid.

I knew, *you* would catch me.

I suppose now would be a good time to tell you another piece of my childhood, to explain a bit more about how we got to where we were then—what better time than in the middle of a dramatic moment, right?

Truly, I'm sorry for the poor timing, but…

I grew up in a small, beautiful home a few streets away from a quiet road that'd one day become far too busy. In a once little town that existed in another world than yours. Where a little girl learned how to see a man she shouldn't have logically been able to know, and to trust him as the knight who would always keep her safe. A guardian who would protect her from anything that may ever try to hurt her. A knight who's always been that little girl's everything, from her first breath of life…

But, you know that very well, already.

In the waking world, that I have yet to really talk about, back then you would come to me in two ways: as your spirit, and your physical being. In a way that will likely be confusing to those who haven't seen life through our eyes. But, when you and I began to see each other in the waking world, we saw one another how we truly were at that current place in time, as I've said previously; and, in some instances, we were shown *us* but older, for when we got to the age where we started to question things.

You see, between the ages of five and six, our dreams started to be seen through the eyes we see through now. Seeing ourselves as we *would* be, when we'd finally cross paths in reality, two decades later. In dreams we'd been grown, I mean, but awake we were kids. I truly hope that makes some sense, because I say this now in hope that the memory I'll explain next will make more sense, too, by explaining this first.

But, I know it already will to you… as impossible as it is to others.

Anyway, back then, you were a secret part of my life. One I had tried to share with those around me many times, throughout my childhood: of course, you know that my family accepted it—especially mom: who I thank with all my heart—they've always accepted me entirely as I am, somehow, even the parts that they aren't able to fully comprehend. But, it was a side I'd learned to hide from the rest of the world when I realized that it's something which makes me different from everyone else... and how much "different" things scare most.

Different in a way only one other will ever understand—you, obviously.

But, at the time of *this* memory, which happened three years before I entirely hid that side from the world, I had been given a small ray of hope that all I knew was true. A ray of hope that's kept me from ever believing our truth is false, or untrue. And, it wasn't even because another saw as I did, or even necessarily believed me, but because it let me see how strongly *I* knew it was true.

You see, you were always the friend only I could see, and yet the only friend I truly ever needed or wanted—besides my sister, Katie.

It was on a day like any other, when I was only five or six. When I'd been sitting on the edge of my bed playing, lost in a world no one else could see. When she—the best sister in the world, and don't let her tell you otherwise—had been the one to ask me a question, to give that ray of hope. She'd pulled me out of our secret world by asking, "Who're you talking to?"

I was startled by it. By the thought that someone heard me talking to you at all: I'd tried so hard not to be overheard, you know. She was standing in the doorway to my room when my eyes met hers, her face carrying a look of confusion and curiosity.

"No one." My voice came out softly, as she started to walk closer, my eyes falling back down to my toys as if I didn't understand.

I'd been afraid she would ask more, since I promised you a long while before that I wouldn't say who you were to anyone. I could talk *of* you, as I certainly do, but only carefully and vaguely: you hadn't wanted the world to call me crazy… as it titled you. That's why I write all of this while omitting your name, or any details such as that, as I'm sure you've noticed. To keep my promise, but still give, at least, enough for you to know I *am* me without question.

Anyway, back then, a part of me hoped she *would* ask, that I could truly share our beautiful secret with another: my sister was the only one I ever really wanted to share that secret entirely with. Still, all I said was, "Just playing."

"You *were* talking to someone." She stopped right at the foot of my bed, her brows creeping higher up her forehead, making her already big eyes seem bigger, wider. She held those brows high, in question, her arms crossed, "Who was it? I won't tell."

I considered for a long time, studying her face to see if she meant it or not, before I slowly set my toys aside. Toys, I should add, who I'd been pretending were us as we talked, knowing telepathy even when we didn't know what it was: as a girl who can see spirits, it's a normal thing to do. "Promise?"

"Sure."

I bit my bottom lip for a second, speaking quietly, "My friend."

"Your imaginary friend?" Her brows began to lower, watching me come down from my bed, walking over to the desk in my room's corner.

"He's not *imaginary*. If he *is*, I wouldn't be able to *talk* to him."

"He's still invisible... How's he real if he doesn't look like anything?"

"*I* see him."

"And?"

"And, *what?*"

"What's he look like?"

"Um..."

"You don't know, do you?"

"He's... pretty. To me. I guess." My mind had lit up as it always does when I talk of you, busy pulling out the desk's chair. Doing what I had the day before, when I'd been alone with you. "His eyes are sad... but *so* pretty."

I climbed onto the chair, grabbing a pencil from the desk as I clambered up to stand on its surface. My then short body having to stretch to hold the pencil up to my closet door, "He's *this* tall. Strong, like daddy, but not as heavy. He protects me."

She only sighed, "Get down... You don't have good balance."

I hopped down from the desk carelessly, rolling my eyes even when she was right. I wobbled when I landed, barely keeping my footing. I ignored it as I usually tended to. Talking quickly, almost too fast to understand as I also tend to, "Calls me a princess. Says he's a knight sent to protect me. From nightmares. He knows I've a lot of those. Knows everything, I guess. I mean, I *tell* him everything... I think he lives in the stars, that's why we talk better at night. On the moon, maybe... we race in this grassy place. He usually wins, but lets me and tries to pretend he doesn't. Dunno why. He's nice, I guess. When I look, before sleeping, I *see* him on the moon. On a horse. It's all—"

"But," She released a heavy breath, "You *know* he's not real."

My brows drew together, stubbornly: offended she doubted you. My hands finding my hips, "He's my *friend*."

"He can be your 'friend' but imaginary."

"He's *real*."

"He's not. Or, I'd have one, too." She let her arms fall free of being crossed, some pity crossing her face when she saw sadness over mine. Not sadness because I thought she was right, as she likely thought, but because she hadn't wanted to believe me.

I knew you *were* real, believing she just didn't *want* to see as I could.

She shook her head, "Mom said dinner's ready. I won't tell... it's okay to pretend."

"'Kay." I went to leave the room before her, my steps skipping, a wide smile across my face. "But, you'll see. He says he'll find me. So, I *promised* to wait. To be patient. You'll see. One day. When I'm a lady, I know he'll come. He *always* does."

It's a promise I always kept, never once thinking of breaking it no matter how hard the endless waiting seems. Even when I doubted my sanity a few times, rather it really were true or imaginary as everyone said, I never lost faith in *you*. Faith in the fact that, if I could only wait to become your "lady," you'd somehow find a way.

Because, you *always* come for me, don't you?

My world snapped back into itself as I once again collided with hard Earth. Landing on my back, as I had before, only this time without your hand to save my head from cracking against the ground after my body. The impact making stars dance before my eyes, even in a world of complete darkness. As a surge of pain, rolling from my skull all the way down to my toes, blessedly returned feeling to my numb body.

Waking instincts that urged me to quickly find my hands and knees as soon as my head struck that hard ground, despite the swirling of my mind. Trying desperately to rise to my feet, but falling a good many times before I was able to find them: trying to run anywhere I could that was *away* from there. But, I only made it a step before my world tipped upside down.

I heard the cry escape my lips. Felt the hand—a cold shadow I shouldn't be able to feel, but felt distinctly of bones—roughly take hold of my waist, yanking me off my feet to throw me harshly, back first, against something. Something that some distant part of my brain knew felt like a tree: a cold, *empty* tree. Its tough, sharp bark drawing another cry from my lips, making me try to push from the tree as soon as I met it. But, it shoved me back hard enough to push every breath from my lungs, to make my eyes once again dance with stars as my head hit the trunk.

Its face was in front of mine when my vision returned, drawing a startled scream from me at the sight: a skull made entirely of thick smoke is the only way to describe it, with endless black hollows for eyes, showing the soul of a being who lacks one, who lacks any *good*.

I regained my sense as it leant closer. And, before I could fully process it, my palm slammed right into the side of its face to shove it away. My body trying to twist away as a hot, stinging fire settled over my hand: its face unyielding, so hard it sent a sharp pang of agony up my wrist, its face harder than my hand; catching my hurt wrist in that boney hand before the shock of pain could travel up my arm. As its other hand snapped around my side with a suffocating hold, its fingers cutting into the tender space between my ribs in a way that nearly made my body fold over.

And, I would have, if it hadn't pinned me tighter to that tree.

"Be still, patient girl." It spoke, far too close to my face. Filling my breaths with its smoke, and an impossible to describe but absolutely horrible smell: the best I can do, is say it smelt like someone burning something rancid. Stopping what little breath I could find, as I tried to yank my hands free. Which only made its hold tighten more, pulling a whimper from my lips as a sick grin twisted on that skull. Its voice seeming to *crawl* over me, "Shh, sweet girl. There's no where to be, silly girl. *Time* is mine, now. It's all right, now, just let me *show* you, little girl."

It edged closer, to make our faces even nearer, until all I felt was ice. I again tried to twist out of its hold, a yelp leaving my lips when something popped as the pressure of its hold tightened. "Shh, quiet girl. Just *relax*. I *will* show you... just share your light, shining girl... And, you will be quiet... a silent girl."

Light: the single word that can lead anyone away from darkness.

A little word that made my eyes snap tightly closed, reaching for a world beyond the dark, *becoming* the beacon you can always see from miles away.

The shadow pulled me away from the tree the moment my eyes closed, trying to throw me back-first to the ground, to stop me from calling out for you. But, somehow my body was prepared, spinning to land on my knees. When it tried to grab me, to push me down, my hand once again connected to its face. Only, this time meeting it with a fist to where a nose should be, shoving it at least enough away for me to find my feet before its hands caught ahold of my arms, from behind, to stop me from doing just the same to it once more.

It didn't realize that's what I'd hoped it would do.

"You're *mine*, selfish girl." It spoke through teeth I couldn't see, as it tried to stop me from fighting. Trapping me in its arms to hold my back against its chest, my arms pinned across *my* chest. It spoke into my ear, "I'll show you—"

It nearly lost its balance when I suddenly stopped fighting, giving me the second I needed to let my eyes fall back closed. For my mind to snap into yours: I saw where you were, heard the thudding of your perfect heart pounding like a maddened drum. I saw, that you could see *me*.

Your light.

"*Run*." I heard that single word, *your* word, rumble through my mind as my head snapped back, cracking against the face behind me: just as you had long ago taught me how to. Twisting easily out of its hold, as it started to fall down to the ground...

And, well, I was long gone before it *hit* that ground.

Silence crashed through the trees just as I shoved it away: that was how I'd barely begun to run as you caught me, leaning over the side of your horse to be even with my height, trusting Silence to stay steady as long as you needed.

Your hand, gentle despite the speed, catching ahold of my waist as the shadow fell to the Earth behind us, lifting me from the ground and onto that horse directly in front of you. Urging Silence to go faster, as you turned us sharply into a new and untouched part of the woods. Guiding us to a place where *they* would be less likely to follow, as your arm wound protectively around me. As your warm body hunched over mine, like a shield, to cover all of me. To let me feel safe, as I only ever feel with you.

"I got you." You kissed the top of my head as my body nestled tighter to yours, as close as I could be. "S'alright."

It always is, somehow, with you.

I wrapped my arms around your waist to hold you to me, my hands locking together at the opposite side of your ribs, but doing so delicately. I was still very aware it was where you were hurt, feeling the terrible wetness of blood soaking through your shirt: wanting more than anything to mend whatever hurt you, and desperately upset by how I currently lacked the ability to do anything about it.

My face turned into your chest, softly kissing over your heart. Saying one word, a single word that is my whole world: your name.

"I've got you, baby." Your gentle hold tightened around me,

laying your hand over my stomach to draw me closer. Letting me feel your magnificent warmth all around me, through me. A part of me. Letting steadier breaths run through both my lungs, and yours. "M'not going anywhere... neither are you."

I freed one of my hands to rest beside my face on your chest, my palm over your heart, to feel your steadiness. Your calm, despite everything. A slower breath running through me, my eyes falling contentedly closed, as you slowly swept your thumb, so amazingly tenderly, across my stomach: a simple touch that somehow conveyed your every feeling, sending a beautiful warmth through me that left no doubt to how safe I was.

How safe *we* were.

A touch that turned my voice into a quiet sigh. How on Earth you heard, I'll never know, "I did alright?"

"Alright?" You kissed the top of my head, staying there as you spoke to let the slow vibration of your words travel through me. "Baby, you're... *truly*, the bravest I know."

"Mm..." I tilted my face up to see yours. And, you lifted your chin to let me, when I did. "You're the bravest in the *world*."

You grunted, "M'far from that."

"In *my* world, Love." My hand slid up your chest, to let my fingertips feather across the under-side of your chin. My nails scratching gently through the coarse hair of your beard—always kept barely grown, really just stubble, as you know I like it to be—as I knew *you* liked me to touch you. "You're everything."

"And, you," You released the reigns to catch my hand within your own, lifting mine to softly kiss my knuckles. Skimming tenderly down the length of my fingers to kiss the tip of each in turn, speaking in between every kiss. First you kissed the tip of my index finger, followed by my thumb, "Are *my* everything." Kissed my pinkie, winking as a giggle left me. "*All* of you," you kissed the middle, "is m'world. And, I *vow*," you kissed my ring finger last, the ring it held, "Nothing'll ever take y'away from me."

I've worn that ring in the land of dreams since I was fifteen, when you first asked me to marry you: the most beautiful ring in the world. But, since our first day alive, to our eyes we already were; we always have been.

"Mm..." I brought our entwined hands down to *my* lips, kissing your knuckles as you had to mine. That smile twitching over your lips as I lowered your hand to be in front of my breasts, over my heart, my thumb brushing across your knuckles. "Tell me honestly... are you doing okay?"

"Jus' fine." You shifted to test your hurt side, trying to hide the cringe that crossed your face: I narrowed my eyes, but your smile quirked higher, your eyes flitting over every part of my face. Saying my appearance wasn't exactly without memory of what happened, either. "And, you? Y'alright?"

I tightened my hand around yours, "Have you, don't I?"

"Always, don't you?" You freed your hand of mine to brush hair from my face, the very second it blew in your way to block your sight of me. Sweeping it tenderly back behind one of my ears as my hand came back to find your heart. Letting you study me freely, as I only let you: unable to stop you from making me see through your eyes, as you showed me that I really am, to you, as beautiful as I only *feel* around you.

This will be the nearest I come to describing appearances, I promise, but I do have to say at least this. How, in more ways than one, sometimes it seems as though we are truly just looking into a mirror, when we see one another. A mirror where we see only the best parts of ourselves. And, while we do have similarities in appearances —mostly only varying in my feminine, and your masculine differences—somehow more than that, this "mirroring" can be seen in how we hold ourselves, and how we *express* ourselves. Possessing many mannerisms, expressions, even phrases, that come solely from each other, and can't be explained any other way.

But—my point in mentioning this here—even when we know just how similar we appear, we still tend to look at our *own* faces entirely differently... unless we see, *with* each other. For instance, you see my face as if it's a perfect face of an angel, but I only see a blotchy, strange face that never looks quite right. Unless, *you* are looking at me: then, I truly feel I *am* as you see me.

Just as you say the same, about how I see you.

So, in this moment where you let me see through your eyes— looking at me with your pure, undeniable love—it startled me. My breaths hitching for a moment before I leant into your touch, turning to softly kiss your sensitive inner-wrist at its most tender point, my eyes looking right into yours in the very same way.

With my own undoubtable love.

"M'yours, my beautiful Danie," It left your lips as that low rumble of thunder, traveling straight from your lips all the way down to the sacred feminine part of me. Your soft breath, ruffling the hair around my face, making my eyes fall closed as a content sigh left my own lips. "*Always* yours, my beautiful everything."

You caught a stray curl of my hair as it tried to slip free under your breath, gently twisting it around the tips of your fingers before you tenderly tucked it behind my ear to join the rest, more lovingly than such a little thing should be able to be. The backs of your knuckles feathering over my cheekbone as your touch slowly drew away: the softness of my skin gliding beneath the perfect roughness of yours. A touch that made my cheek, and your hand ignite with the vibrant, nearly overwhelming current that we only feel with one another.

The indescribable current of *Love*.

Letting your palm softly rest over my cheek, seeking the feeling of my skin. Of me. Just as badly as I sought the feeling of you. Your thumb tenderly feathering across my bottom lip, getting my chin to lift as you leant down to rest your forehead right against mine. To see only my eyes, as I saw yours. The perfect sea, which is my everything. I didn't notice the tears starting to tumble down my cheeks until your gentle thumb rose to catch them as they fell: as your other hand tightened, protectively, around my waist to erase the *wrongness* of someone else's touch.

And, I didn't realize I was shaking, until the sob left my lips in place of the words I tried to form: a sob that was only able to speak your name.

"Hey… s'alright." Your body folded around mine, tilting your face down beside my own, almost upside down. Letting your lips slowly, tenderly, travel up the side of my face: your breath sending soft, beautiful warmth across my neck, making goosebumps rise across my skin, taking away all memory of the ice. "I've *got* you, baby."

Your kiss feathered across my chin, my cheeks, everywhere except my lips. Your beard gently scratching my skin, *warming* my skin, as you kissed your way down the side of my throat: trying to erase the fear we'd both had when parted.

"I'm sorry," My arms tightened around you, making your hold tighten more, too, protective as no one else can possibly be. My body curling somehow tighter to yours, when such a thing should have been impossible. "I couldn't… I didn't know…"

"I know, baby. I know." One of your arms briefly left me, finding the under-side of my knees to lift my legs over yours, to where I had been struggling to get them on my own. Your arm wrapping fully back around me just as soon as it had left, surrounding all of me with all of you. "But, you're safe now."

Again, I only spoke your perfect name.

"I know." You kissed my throat, in that soft, tender way it's impossible to describe the love within. "You're *safe*, baby."

My body relaxed against yours, as I only ever can with you, seeming to meld right into you. Trusting your words entirely. I spoke softly, at a volume that shouldn't have been audible, but of course you, my Everything, heard me. "With *you*, I am."

I truly *always* am, with you.

We stayed that way for a long while, simply holding one another. Just how long I'll never know exactly, but it must've been quite long by the distance we travelled. And, when I *did* draw my face away from your chest, you automatically lifted your own to let my eyes find yours, knowing what I sought. Letting me show you every thought in my mind: our eyes shining, every emotion laid bare, as eyes can only be when looking into the eyes that equal their whole world.

When nothing else matters.

My hand slowly came from over your shoulder to find the side of your face, my palm held softly over your cheek as my thumb swept tenderly across your skin. Still covered in dirt and dust, with the many fine cuts dashed over your face barely visible through the grime, yet all I saw was the pure magnificent beauty hidden beneath.

I saw you as you *really* are, just as you saw me.

My lips parted to say that one word as you leant into my hand. A hand that seemed small, delicate, beside your own. A single word said in a very specific way. A way that I knew held the power to make your entire world tilt suddenly on its axis... because it did the same to me when *you* spoke that way.

You answered with one of those grunts of many meanings, "Mm?"

I hadn't realized how close you had leant down until we spoke, our breaths merging as one, your forehead tight against mine. Tilting my chin, so my lips were just shy of touching yours, "Are we alone?"

A smile twitched faintly across those lips, "We are."

"Nothing followed us?"

"Impossible." Your smile grew to reveal one of your perfect canines. In the way my body always reacts to, and likely more than it should: you pretended you didn't notice when I shifted against you, even when it was obvious you did. "Why d'you ask?"

"Curious." I tried to ignore how my voice was higher than it should be, but the glint in your eye didn't. "Was there more to your plan than getting away?"

That smile quirked on the other side, "Jus' followed the nearest road."

"You didn't *follow* a road, Love."

"Didn't I?" You slightly widened your perfect, sparkling eyes, lifting your brows as you glanced around. In a way that successfully drew a laugh from me. "Shit. Must've gotten lost."

"You're never lost, Darling. Your brain's a compass."

"Are you saying... I brought us here *intentionally*?" You slowed Silence down to a calm, *very* slow walk, showing how sure you were that we *were* alone. "Somewhere no one else knows the whereabouts to?"

"Mhm." That smile crossed my face, the one that always makes *your* body react. I, however, didn't pretend not to notice. "Would've been such a perfect plan."

"Would it?" You quirked one of your brows. Your own smile lifting in unison, and exposing both canines. As your eyes, those *beautiful* eyes, started to glitter just like the stars with pure happiness: a magnificent sight, that makes it truly impossible for me to deny you anything, even if I want to.

So, it's a good thing I'll never want to...

"Mhm." My fingertips brushed slowly across your cheekbones, sweeping your soft hair behind your ears. All except the strands that hung between your brows, over the bridge of your perfect nose. Something I do frequently, which always makes a nearly goofy grin cross your face, crinkling the skin around your magnificent eyes.

Letting my thumb feather over your lips as my other fingertips delicately traced the fine lines that divine smile created. The smile I would truly do absolutely anything to conjure. I kissed you softly: my eyes staying on yours, watching them instantly dilate for me, saying just how much you wanted, and needed me. Letting my hand slide into the hair at the back of your neck, drawing you down closer to let me kiss you deeper, harder; letting me show you just how much I wanted to give.

My tongue parting your lips to find your own, shy as I always am at first. Slow, and light, as we started to dance in a smooth, gentle rhythm. Gently, and slowly, until your hand found the nape of my neck to tilt my head back, to deepen the kiss, letting our pace become more urgent. Kissing me roughly, and yet somehow gently, as your hand at my waist—its arm wrapped around my back—lifted me just enough to allow one of my legs to move to the other side of you, my ankles crossing behind you. Getting a growl to rumble through your chest when I moved my hips against yours, just so: the sound that always makes the muscles deep in my belly answer to you.

My hand tangled into your hair to bring you further down to me, taking and giving you everything. Only drawing away to regain breath, an inch and not a bit more: our eyes saying a thousand words without truly speaking one… but, of course, I said three anyway, "I love you."

Those words made that vibrant smile return to your beautiful face, your perfect eyes glittering for me, declaring love to a deeper extent than words ever could. Your lips finding mine, briefly and sweetly, before you rested your forehead against my own. To see how my eyes sparkled back.

Seeing all the way to my very spirit, as only you can.

"I love *you*." Your hand, tangled deep in *my* hair, massaged the back of my neck to tilt my face further up to yours, keeping my forehead against yours, our noses beside the other. As your other hand glided slowly, tenderly, down to find one of my hips, holding me to you: letting me feel how much you meant your words. "And, I *want*... *need* you, baby."

Your name left my lips, as a quiet whisper. My hand finding your heart, erratically pounding against my palm. A heart that beat in perfect time with my own. Letting my hand slowly close over you, gently drawing down the neck of your shirt to allow my nails to softly brush over your skin. Through the soft hair on your chest, as I know you like me to. Feeling that heart skip. "My Love, I'm *yours*. And, you—"

You kissed me, slowly and deep, "*Only* yours."

Silence walked entirely on his own as though he knew where you would want us to be. Calmly taking us away from the danger of before as we lived in our private world, oblivious to anything else. The path he lead us down was winding, guided by gentle curves of a river. A river that must span at least thirty feet across, with its water softly rippling under a slow current, splitting gently around stray stones speckled through its path. On the other side was the forest you rarely let the horse step out from, that we rarely leave when in dreams where we are alone.

A safe haven most others were unable to find.

The long branches of its dense trees curved high overhead toward the river as if it longed to reach what it never would far on the other side, blanketing the narrow bank we followed in cool shade, adding to the already chilled air before the storm.

Silence travelled along that river slowly, making the journey take three times what it should have as if he knew how much time we would need: and, I didn't doubt it was so. When we reached where the horse had been headed, when we had the conversation just shared shortly above, the sun had by then risen up to the middle of the sky, the dream-time nearing noon.

But, I suppose, time didn't matter…

It was as we parted to say those words that the horse had turned away from the river to follow a small creak weaving deeper into the forest, following a tight path between a cliff-side, and that gentle little creak. A cliff whose upper ridge was lined by trees, reaching to grab hold of those on the other side, at the river's edge, their entwined branches creating an arch over the hidden path.

Hiding the way from any who may pass by.

Just as the horse came to a stop at a gentle bend of that little creak, where its water cascaded calmly down that cliff-side, you untangled your hand from my hair, freeing it to find my behind. Lifting me entirely off the horse's back. As Silence leant down to start nibbling at the grass at the water's end, you dismounted from the horse with my body cradled securely against yours. Doing so with far more ease than one should be able to: an ease undoubtedly granted by being so involved with love you didn't know what you were doing otherwise.

You set me on my feet as soon as you landed on your own, keeping my body tightly to yours, our lips dancing in that graceful rhythm of love. Using your body to back me slowly up to rest my back against the smooth bark of a tree along the water's edge, meeting my eyes as I met its trunk, to see if our world was about to crash back into the waking one.

I spoke softly, breathless, "We're still here."

"Yeah." You kissed me, quickly and sweetly: continuing to do the very same to every last inch of my face. Making a giant smile spread widely across my well-loved face in response. "We are."

"You don't think—"

You interrupted me with another kiss, "No."

"But, it's possible after—"

Another. "No."

"It usually means we—"

"Baby, no." Your hands rose to cup either side of my face, letting the tip of your nose touch mine. Getting my smile to grow. "I'm *here*. Aren't I?"

"You certainly are." My hand caught ahold of your belt, drawing you even closer, until all that stood between that part of you and me was my hand. I rose up onto my toes, kissing you once, slowly. "*Right* here. But, if we... we might wake. And..." My eyes fell down to your nose, instead of your eyes, "I don't want to lose you."

"*Right* here, y'said." You leant your forehead against mine, those eyes shining with a vow. A vow that I knew would never be broken. "We're *both* right here."

"But—"

"But, nothing." Your thumbs glided slowly down my cheeks to find my jawline, making sure I saw the sincerity shining in your irises. "M'not going anywhere."

My hand released your belt, sliding to your unhurt side as the other found your fast heart. Looking at you with mirroring sincerity, "Don't let me wake up, either."

That beautiful smile quirked over your lips, "I won't."

You kissed me in that almost rough way, deeply, catching me as my lips were parted to say something more. Making my legs forget I had knees at all, just as one of your hands caught the small of my back, pulling my chest securely against your own. With both of my hands finding *your* chest, your perfect heart, right as you had pinned them there: hearing a soft, very happy moan leave my lips as you did.

A small sound that made you kiss even *more* passionately, which should've been impossible. Making us truly lose all thought of anything outside one another: it was simply your warm body against mine; your strong hands holding me to you, without any assistance from me; the beautiful heat of your sweet mouth connecting with mine, dancing with an understanding few truly have.

Knowing the other far better than ourselves.

Letting your other hand leave my face to glide tenderly down my back, finding my behind to lift me higher. Making me instinctively rise onto my toes, going just where and as you wanted me: telling you that you could really do whatever you may want, giving you complete and total freedom over me.

Showing you that all I have is yours, if you only ask.

A moan escaped you as I did so. As you pulled my pelvis forward to hold my hips tighter against yours, as close as possible. Moaning again as my nails softly scratched at your scalp, as a mirroring sound went through me, clutching your hair like a lifeline, moving my hips not-so-subtly against yours. Another groan, nearly a growl, rumbling through you as your strong hand tightened on my behind, lifting me higher: letting *you* find *me*, to be as near as we could be with our clothes still between us.

An answering—even happier—moan leaving me as your hips moved against mine, even less subtly: the muscles in my belly and below magnificently igniting as my body reacted to yours. As you lifted me the rest of the way from the ground, your hand leaving my behind to find one of my thighs, wrapping my legs around your hips as you started to gather my skirt in your hand. Pushing the skirt higher, out of your way, to let your hand find the bare skin of my thigh. Caressing me as your tender touch ventured further, supporting my weight on your forearm instead of that hand: letting the warmth of your touch find that place I never let anyone else find, drawing a soft gasp from my lips.

Making that near growl leave you, your kiss becoming more urgent; preparing to take us away from that tree, to lower us down to the soft Earth and make me truly yours, to be truly *one*.

But, then… you *dropped* me.

I felt your body tense, just before it happened. Before a new sort of growl, the deep sort of pain, tore through you: before your left hand lost all feeling, and lost the hold it possessed of me, falling without feeling down to your side. I'd barely had time to drop my feet to the ground as you, nearly, doubled over—if not for the tree, and me, you would have—wrapping my arms around your waist as your legs weakened, keeping you from falling entirely.

Holding you as you leant heavily against me, your fast breaths pounding against the side of my throat, unable to be caught. I wouldn't have been able to keep us standing without the help of that tree; nearly failing when all your weight fell limp in my arms. When your head rolled into the curve of my throat, your heavy breath turning to blow across my shoulder.

When you, my Everything, actually lost consciousness.

That single word—your perfect name—left my lips, blatantly carrying all my fear and worry. And, I felt your head shift in the crook of my throat at the sound. A faint groan leaving you as one of your hands clumsily, heavily, lifted onto the shoulder that your head wasn't on, in an attempt to ease my worry. But, you were only able to find it for a moment before that strong hand tightened around me, far beyond your control, as your entire body tensed under a new wave of pain.

Loosening your hand the second after, your fingers gently massaging the back of my neck in apology as you planted your other previously immovable hand against the tree at my side, trying to support some of your weight. I slid an arm lower down your back when you did, to let you: knowing if I took any weight back, you'd only be upset at yourself for not being able to on your own. Even when I undoubtedly felt the warm wetness that found my forearm at the slightest contact.

I released the breath I hadn't known I'd been holding, "How bad is it?"

"M'alright." You grunted, shifting to try supporting more weight, but ending up as you started. Grunting all over again when I went to help you more. "M'fine."

"No, you aren't." I drew my face away from yours, asking you to do the same. You did, lifting your head slowly: to let me see a face pale as I had only seen it a few times before, devoid of color; your eyes unable to focus on mine. "*Sit* down. Let me see."

"Yes, ma'am." An extremely lopsided smile crossed your lips, your eyes flicking away from mine to see the edge of the water, lined by a few high stones. One was just a foot away, and before I could stop you, you fell somehow gracefully down to sit.

Even if you *did* nearly tip over once you'd landed.

I caught you before you could, finding your either shoulder. My eyes narrowing on yours as I knelt in front of you, "Let's try *not* to fall in the river, yeah?"

You smirked, again totally lopsidedly, "S'not a'river."

"Love," I kissed your nose, "I'm being serious."

"Mm… M'serious woman, I'll not b'falling anywhere." This was a moment where, if I didn't talk to you all the time, your accent would've been impossible to decipher: slurring in pain as if you were drunk. "Y'found m'worse many times, was jus' fine."

"Hardly the point..." I released your shoulder only once I was sure you could stay upright. Watching as you *very* slowly leant forward to rest your elbows on your knees, burying your face in your hands with your fingers tugging at your hair: giving me full permission to do whatever I had to. And, I shifted over to your left side as soon as you did so, letting my eyes find the darkened part of your shirt, where the gray had turned a reddish-brown. As my hands gingerly rolled its hem up to the height of your ribs, to let my fingertips delicately feather below and around the wound.

Across skin that had started to turn dark, *dark* purple.

My eyes lifted onto the side of your face as my fingertips probed you, to make sure I wasn't hurting you, but a faint cringe was the only response you gave. A sign which could either mean you felt just a touch of pain, or that you stubbornly refused to show a greater pain and a cringe was all that got by your control: and, knowing you, I knew it leant to the latter.

So, my eyes fell to where the cruel shard of slate, inflicting the wound, pierced your waist. A piece that looked like a big knife without a hilt, making a gash that ran about three inches wide: a clean puncture, if it hadn't torn somewhere between when you'd gotten it and then. Which, I knew, had been when you'd forgotten its existence to get to me. Now, it gaped gruesomely open to show how deep it was, how it almost went all the way *through* your waist; but, even that wasn't the sight which worried me the most... it was how it was leaking both a lot of blood and what could only be the start of a serious infection that did.

It was a sight that would've made me look away with anyone else, but that's never the case with you: while I get lightheaded at the sight of a small cut if it's my own, I can study the sight without problem if it's on you, since I'll only see how to possibly mend it. So, as gory as it certainly was, the only reaction I showed—like you—was a cringe, my eyes lifting back to yours.

By then, your head was drooping, eyes hooding, unable to stay fully open.

Making me softly clear my throat: a gentle sound that startled you enough to make your whole body flinch; your eyes blinking a bit more open, but still not near focused. That's why I spoke, too. "Doesn't look as fine as you say, my Love."

You let a hand fall free of your hair, slapping against your calves to create a sound that made me flinch as you had. Tilting your face against the other hand, to let your still swimming eyes find mine, "S'not s'bad as it looks, then."

My eyes narrowed on yours, "Be honest, Darling, please."

"Honest." You lifted your dropped hand to tenderly tuck a stray curl behind my ear, letting two of your fingers skim the underside of my jaw to rest under my chin, gently tilting my face further up to yours. "*I'm* alright. Would tell y'if I wasn't."

"No, you wouldn't." I kissed your wrist, just above your watchband; you know *why* I did so. Shifting to sit on my knees directly in front of you, so suddenly that you leant a bit back in surprise, "You're just lucky I can fix it."

Your eyes narrowed on mine, for reasons I understood but didn't change my mind: because we both know, if we spend too much energy in a dream we'll wake up barely able to function the next day, either depleted of that energy or far worse.

But, you are *far* worth everything.

I shifted closer, until my nose was just touching yours. Until your world was simply my eyes, looking at you in the way I know you can't ever deny, "You're not going to stop me, are you?"

You grunted, "S'not fair, m'dear."

"Nope." A smile crossed my lips, my hands finding your either breast to gently ease you a bit further back. You went where I asked you to be without complaint, knowing there really wasn't a point in arguing. My mind is just as impossible to sway once it's set as yours is. "You're not attached to this shirt are you?"

You quirked a brow, your lips doing the same, "No?"

"Good. I know I *could* simply go to Silence for a bandage, but that'd mean leaving your side, which isn't an option. So…" I caught ahold of the hem on your shirt to start taking it from you. And, you leant further back to help, your hands catching ahold of the fabric beside my own to tug it the rest of the way over your head.

Balling it up for me to take as you settled right back into the position I'd put you in before, a smirk wide across your face. The magnificent one which beautifully crinkles around your sparkling eyes, "Better?"

"Mhm… Bit more distracting, but yeah."

You put a pout over your lips, making a laugh leave me, "Only 'a bit'?"

"Shush. You know you're *far* more than that." I placed that shirt on my knee, my hands finding your either breast: my soft touch sending a shiver slowly over you, as it slid down your chest to find what needed mending. "It isn't... normal is it?"

You grunted, "Nothing t'night is."

"Hm, but that's not necessarily bad." My thumbs brushed across your skin on either side of the slate. A warning of what I was going to do, before I did. "Is it?"

"S'long as they don't—" You grunted as I made my hand yank the stone from your side, quickly replacing it with your shirt in a feeble attempt to slow its bleeding. When you spoke again your voice was rougher, but that's the only sign you gave of the pain you felt. "— come near you."

"They'll try to." My eyes lifted back up to yours, letting my hand flatten over your breast as the other held the shirt tight to the wound. "But, we'll be alright."

"Undoubtedly." A grunt left your lips when I applied more pressure. When I felt the blood hot and wet against my hand. You tried to act like you hadn't reacted, when my eyes softened on yours, "Wanted your light, yeah? S'even brighter tonight."

"They did." My gaze fell down to your hurt side, gingerly lifting the fabric away to see... making my eyes instantly return to yours, glassy despite your best effort: so, I took more of your pain onto myself, as we always do. "But, it's only *yours* to have... and you'll have it, won't you?"

"Far be it from me to say 'no.'" Your words were a grunt, but you winked at me as my eyes fell closed, as a deeper, slower breath left my lips. Watching the light only you can see slowly start to radiate around me.

Staying still as I let my hand lift from your side, leaving only my fingertips to gently feather your skin. Staying still as I shifted closer, my aura wrapping around you as my lips found your heart. Slowly kissing my way across your breasts, your soft hair tickling my lips as I feathered over your skin: trying to take all of your attention away from your hurt side… making your breaths quicken, and your heart thud faster.

You broke your stillness as my lips started higher, your hand rising to find the nape of my neck, as your eyes fell heavily closed.

As my hand skimmed down your chest, to your stomach, and I delicately traced your collar-bone with my tongue. Finding the hollow of your throat just so, in a way that made all of your magnificent body react to the heat following my touch. As my gentle hand softly returned to your side, to where you were hurt: letting my palm tenderly press over the wound, touching you as if afraid you would vanish if I touched you wrong.

Because, a part of me was afraid of just that.

It was a touch that probably should have hurt you more, but instantly took all agony away: because, my palm was warm from my light, and carried my every heartbeat at the slightest touch, carrying the love of my spirit. And, when I let it make contact with that injury I sent all my light *into* you, sending that gentle warmth through your veins, your every nerve, every cell that makes you who and how you are.

Guiding my love through you, to stitch what was broken back together.

Letting my light decipher, and rid you of the mystery behind the agony: the strange poison the slate carried, which had quickly infected your bloodstream when it pierced your skin. Telling us just as the spirit implied, that the Earth itself was hurting down to its core, as every part of the world tilted off-balance; that something had *planned* for the slate to find you, to show us the gravity of that truth, the gravity behind everything we would have to do before the end of that night.

What we had to do, to regain its balance.

And, just how you'd withstood that pain for as long as you had, I'll never know: it really did take all of my energy for that warmth, my light, to take place of the poison. For your breaths to clear, the pulsing in your nerves to ease, your mind to regain its usual steadiness, and the disembodied feeling to leave your limbs.

Only coming back to myself as my eyes rose to find yours, as my fingertips swept delicately across the soft pink line dashed across your side, becoming just as smooth as the rest of your skin. The small cuts across your face vanishing as I lifted my other hand from your stomach to find the side of your perfect face, my fingertips feathering over the slice that had once broken skin beside your nose, becoming a fading line.

Making a small, utterly happy smile cross my lips, "Perfect."

"Yeah." Your hand rose to mirror me, to find the side of my face, letting your thumb sweep tenderly across my cheek. Your beautiful, perfect eyes truly declaring far more love than words can. "*You* are."

"Mm." I leant into your hand, kissing the inside of your wrist. "That's debatable."

"Not t'my eyes, m'dear."

My smile grew, "Only because you're sweet, my Love."

You grunted, "Now, *that's* debatable."

"Not t'my eyes, m'darling." I kissed your wrist again, tilting my face away when you leant forward to meet my lips. Since, I obviously knew what would happen if you did. "But, we've limited time, don't we? Before the storm, I mean. Should get going…"

Your thumb swept over my bottom lip, already tender and swollen from your earlier love, turning my face back to yours. "Don't care 'bout time right now."

"Mm." I kissed your palm, my other hand leaving your waist to find yours on my face. Entwining our fingers as I drew yours down to rest on your knee. "But, there's also the fire, I'm sure that hasn't vanished. And, the shadows…"

You grunted, "You mean, the withering forest."

"The… what?"

You quirked a brow, "Y'didn't see that?"

"Definitely, no. What—"

"Doesn't matter." Your hand left that knee to catch ahold of the side of my waist, drawing me closer to you: making it clear why you didn't care about it just then at that precise moment, had there been a doubt before. "Seemed t'be moving slowly."

"Right…" I couldn't hide the smile across my lips as your eyes tightened on mine, knowing I wasn't done. "But, there's also Katie… I didn't miss the whole part of what was said about 'the one who sees below the soil.' And, I know you didn't either. And, if she's in trouble, we have to help her. Before—"

"She can wait." You leant forward to find my lips, and that time I let you. Kissing me just once, yet slow and deep, your eyes staying on mine. Speaking against my lips in the way which really is a continuous kiss, "Likely not in any trouble."

"*Likely*." I rose before you could kiss me again, and you came with me: your hand staying around my waist to prevent more than even a foot from getting between us as I walked to Silence. "I don't think you'd wait if there was any chance *I* was in trouble."

You grunted, "No fucking chance."

"We won't wait for her, either." You only let us make it to the horse's side, before you stopped me with that hand. And, despite my worry of time, I gratefully leant back into you when you wound that arm around my waist, to draw me securely against your chest: telling me everything *would* be alright.

Because, I knew what the spirit had meant as no one else could.

And, I feel, now is the time to say a touch more about my waking reality…

The best place to begin this piece of the story would likely be when I was ten, and starting to comprehend what love *really* means. And, well, everything that goes along with the feeling. Because—though, of course we have never been merely "friends" at any age… we've always known we're far more than that—when I *was* ten, you kissed me for the first time. On my lips, that is: before, we had shyly kissed cheeks, mostly you to mine, and you've kissed my forehead all my life. But, that day, I asked you what it felt like to *truly* kiss, as a not-so-subtle way to ask you *to* kiss me; and you, of course, said you didn't know and not-so-subtly found the answer with me.

Changing our shy love into *true* young love, that softly cradled us as we found who we were meant to be. That safely surrounded us, and helped us survive when life came crashing in to test us with the cruel trials of the world, when we were barely teens.

It was when I was fourteen that it started: the beginning of a horrible shift, that'd go on for years. Though, you—my brave Love—had already faced a great many trials in your life by then, and it never seemed to stop multiplying for you... in comparison, I have very little to talk about, but it first began when our beloved cat passed away. And then, the month after, my family found out Katie was battling extreme weight loss, as her body itself fought her, trying to tear her apart from the inside.

In ways that made her close off from the world... from me.

But, to avoid going too far into the story of how awful and difficult that time was, since it's simply something I don't want to detail here, I'll only say how I had gone to bed in tears every night, back then; praying the gods and goddesses would show me how to help her in some way, how to *save* her. Terrified of losing my sister, too, but helpless to stop it; questioning what good I even was, if I couldn't protect her.

If I can't protect those I *love*.

And, that was the year when I started to *truly* feel you in the physical world. I'd felt you before, I know it sounds confusing—feels impossible to explain—but until then, I felt your touch as a sort of static: the tickling feeling of electricity feathering over me, as your energy mixed with mine, as my sense of feeling tried to decipher what it was. An unexplainable, beautifully soft warmth over my skin that I couldn't possibly deny was someone or something trying to touch me, just not *true* physical contact.

What one feels, I suppose, when a spirit interacts with them.

But, then, you sent your spirit to me so strongly I could feel your arms around me as I cried, as my heart shattered. As I let only *you* see just how destroyed I was. And, you, my Love, *you* pieced me back together, piece-by-piece, and stronger than before. As *we* grew stronger than before... when you faced horrible challenges in your world, too: but, this isn't the place for me to say what or how.

I know you wouldn't want me to.

So, I'll only say, the struggles we faced quickly turned our budding young love into blossoming adult love. The *feeling*, at least, it was later that we grew into *other* adult activities of love, though sooner than my parents will likely be glad to know.

And, eventually—as you've said, "no matter how dark it seems, the light always comes back"—the awful things of that time slowly began to ease. None of it vanished entirely, of course: my sister still deals with a great deal of it, even now. But, it *did* ease enough to regain some sense of normalcy.

This started when I was fifteen, Katie seventeen... when she first saw our world.

She had been having dreams a month before. Nightmares she didn't understand and couldn't control, of raging smoke chasing her through a forest while she ran away on horseback. Until something made her change her path... and, she broke free to find *us* in a certain field of flowers. If she hadn't recognized me, or remembered all I said as kids at the sight of you, she likely wouldn't have fought to recall. But, when she woke that morning, she sent a text describing what happened in that dream perfectly, just as I'd seen it—opening a door that let us share dreams, and often.

Because, it gave her hope, a *purpose*, she said: a reason to keep living.

Even to this day she can never *see* you after she wakes, she only remembers your presence: she calls you "the wall" for that reason. But, that dream let her see how I'm different at your side, compared to the waking reality: how free I am with you, and how happy. So, she made me start to tell her more about you, though nowhere near everything—as I've said before, I *have* kept that promise. And, she said, after, that I'd healed her by talking of you, pulling her out of seclusion by telling her of our dreams, and what we strove to one day find. It made her determined to help us find our way home... even if our relationship, you and I, is more complicated than simply knowing the other and meeting in the physical world.

She'll never truly know how much it helped me, too. How much confidence she let me find, how much strength I was able to gain, through sharing it with her: just as she found the same through me. My sweet sister, you see—no matter how I try to tell her the truth of it —blames herself for the delay in our meeting, thinking what she went through held me back, but that is the furthest thing from true: if she hadn't helped me find that strength, we wouldn't have been able to learn who *we* are.

Because, in finding confidence, strength and truth in myself, I started to see who *you* truly were, too. Before, as you know, you had wanted me to believe your life was easy and fine, not wanting me to know who or what you were. You were afraid, once I knew, I'd turn my back on you, leave you behind... forget you, as you felt everyone did. You were afraid I'd one day wake up and think you were just a dream, and move on. Or, even worse, I'd see you as you really are and I'd hate you for it.

Because, you thought you weren't *good* enough.

So, when I started to see passed your walls you tried to say what I saw wasn't based in any fact, just random nightmares or images: nothing really true. But, I persisted as I always do, until you finally knew I wasn't going anywhere... and you *showed* me.

Again... I would say more, but here isn't my place to: it's yours.

I'll only say, that I saw the side you feared me hating. The reality and truth of all that happens after you wake; as well as the nightmares that catch you before I come to sleep with you, the visions of that cruel shadow literally tearing you apart... the only nightmares I wake up frightened by, that I wake up in tears after.

But, I was never tempted to run away: seeing *you*, only pulled me *closer* to you.

And, well... that's how when I was nearing sixteen, we'd learned how to make love in the realm of dreams, with a lucid clarity few will be able to truly understand. A clarity that put all thought of wanting that divine connection with any other yet farther from my mind. It was such a perfect night, too: truly the sweetest most beautiful night that a girl could hope or dream of.

The night our relationship grew into the equivalent of true marriage.

And, the perfection of the years following slowly helped me open up to who, and how, and what I really am. What *we* are. Before, I'd known I was "gifted," but I never did know the extent of it. I'd turned away when it became too much to comprehend, when it became too much to live with.

But, I learned to accept it: to live as the strange psychic girl who sees the future at random moments, at the expense of many bowls and plates, dropped when my mind leaves me—unable to even drive without being a hazard—the strange girl who can't touch anyone else, at risk of knowing their spirit at the slightest brush; the strange girl who's known her *own* spirit from the first day of her life, and knows each of her many lifetimes just as well as her present one—lives spent at your side, as you know, trying to find the freedom to love as we're meant to, but consistently torn apart by the forces of a society that couldn't understand—the strange girl who can see *all* the spirits who secretly walk the Earth with us... the girl who has always loved one man with all her heart, even before truly "meeting" you.

But, then it came to being nineteen...

I won't get into the entire situation behind it, only that it had to do with a night where, when I reached out for you, I found a feeling of cold dread in the pit of my stomach. And, the nightmares you had fought away so many years before returned, finding me each time I closed my eyes for many horrible weeks: nightmares where we'd constantly tried to fight our way back together, to find light in the darkness; but, only found brief—perfect—moments, as we broke through the horror to make it back to each other, just as we had as kids. Perfect little minutes that made us forget the nightmares of before, that made everything else worthwhile.

At least, until I started to learn *why* it was happening.

It has never been a hidden thing, that you've always blamed yourself for the "gifts" I have. And, of course, you *are* the cause to everything I am, including the extent of *what* I am. But, we both know I can say the same about who and what you are: all of that is my "fault," too.

Everything we are, is because of the other.

But, during that struggle at nineteen, you started to blame yourself as never before: it made your mind go to places it should never go, an agony I felt as my own pain and fear, as your world fell into the nightmares of *your* mind, too. And, I was helpless to take that awful pain away… to save you. Until, one sunrise after a particularly awful night, I learned the extent of how deep you had fallen into the darkness.

A night worse than any before: because I felt myself *losing* you.

I learned one morning in a wave of panic, when you said something that told me the root of why things were happening as they were. And I, in utter fear, had begged my parents to take me to the emergency room, to prove the pain wasn't happening to me, to show *you* it wasn't me: that it was a feeling of hopelessness, from *you*.

It was the day I became determined to do absolutely *anything* I had to do in order to break back through those walls, once and for all… as I did, in the end, with my voice. I suppose that will sound strange, to most. But, all our life I've done the same thing when you're scared: when either of us are sad or simply don't have the words to say, I sing to you, instead. Because, you say my voice, my words, hold the calming power to ease whatever hurts you—that's why I'm using *words* to call for you, now.

Because, back then, my voice lead you home, too.

Our nightmares started to end when I had been watching a movie in the living room with my parents—what movie it was I couldn't tell you, my mind wasn't there—when a horrible pain shot through me. The worst sort of fear, sickness and agony I ever felt before and will likely ever again.

Because, I knew what it meant.

Before the pain had time to fully register, I'd ran up to my room to send my spirit to you. Breaking down the walls between us easily in my fear, because I knew if I didn't, I'd *lose* you: I found you when you'd been about to end the life I love more than any other. When the darkness had convinced you doing so was the only way to "free" me. Only stopping, you said, when you heard me saying how, if you left this life, I would leave right along with you—which I undoubtedly would.

Because, there's no *life* for us without the other.

That was the night we learned the power of my light: all our lives we've been able to heal one another from a distance, but that night we'd learned the extent of Love's power. How it can banish any darkness, can save any life cruelty tries to take away: how even when it seems impossible, love can always bring back the light.

So, while I've called what happened at nineteen "darkness," I suppose that's really not true. That year allowed us to find the light inside of us. It let us find and know the truth of our spirits: that nothing can tear apart two souls who are already one. It's true there *was* darkness, and the worst sort of agony. Especially, in the nights we couldn't reach one another. But, every time we *did*, my beautiful Love, it truly was everything. And, without it we never would have found how true everything is.

How true *we* are.

Which, presently, has lead me to open up to Katie more than before. Talking about you until my parents started to listen and *truly* believe, too. As it lead you, my clever man, to find ways to give me hints to find you once the time came, hints that nothing could stop me from hearing or seeing. Small things to piece together over time, little words or hidden signs that'd likely seem insignificant to most, but mean everything.

So, you see, that darkness let us find the light to find our way *home*.

And—my reason for telling this just now—my sister, I knew, wasn't going to let anything stop us from succeeding: it didn't matter what may stand in her way, she'd destroy any obstacle between us and her goal.

So, I knew what the spirit in the quarry meant… as no one else could.

You caught my chin gently between your thumb and index finger to tilt my face up to yours, tipping my head back against your shoulder, "Nothing's going t'hurt you."

I easily turned in your arms. My hands sliding up to find the sides of your throat, to bring you closer to me: to show who I *was* worried about, had it been unclear. "You know I'm not worried about *me*, Love."

"I know." You leant down to rest your forehead against mine. Letting the warmth of your breath spread softly across my face, "But, as I said, nothing's going t'hurt you. *Or* your sister."

"Or *you*, yeah?"

"None a'us." You let your perfect nose nuzzle against mine, your eyes softening in the vow nothing could ever break. "Everything'll be alright, m'light. Always is."

"Mhm." I let my lips brush over yours with my words, "Because of *you*."

You made that grunt, "'Cause a'us, y'mean."

"Mostly you." I rose onto my toes to let my chin find yours. My lips staying against yours, to make your smile quirk higher, "The shadows tend to forget, I'm protected by the most amazing, kind, strong, beautiful man who ever has or will exist."

Your brows furrowed, as if it really didn't, "Doesn't sound like me."

"Well, I don't share dreams like ours with anyone else… so, it has to be."

"No. Y'better not." You lifted your forehead from mine, your hands encircling my waist as you leant slightly back. Letting your eyes study my face, as if I were hiding something. "Would have t'hunt him down… wouldn't be pretty." You leant further, to see all of me, "Though… it *does* look pretty from here."

An unexpected laugh left me, getting that smile to quirk over your lips, "You really *are* a dork sometimes."

You lifted a brow, "Am I?"

"Mhm." I rose higher onto my toes to kiss your chin, unable to reach you otherwise now that you pulled away. "We already agreed, my sweet dork."

"Maybe... but, I mean it. You, *my* Life," You leant down to kiss my forehead, as amazingly tenderly as always, "Better not dream of anyone else like this."

"Well, I assure you, my Love, I'd *never* dream of it." I kissed the tip of your nose, able to reach now that you had leant down, getting that smile of yours to grow into its almost goofy state. The smile that softly crinkles the skin around your perfect eyes. "Honestly, why would I? I mean... I *do* only feel safe with you. Even if you always *do* get yourself hurt to protect me, when you really *should* protect yourself."

You grunted, "Your life's far more important than mine."

"Uh, no. *You* are far, far more important than I'll ever be."

Again, you grunted, "Not even close."

"You're right, it's *not* close. So, shush. I wasn't done." I let my arms slide over your shoulders, my hands clasped at the nape of your neck to draw you closer to my height when you tried to lift away. "You give me all the confidence in the world: I've always known I can't possibly disappoint you."

You made that perfect grunt, "Impossible. You're perfect."

"I'm far from that. But, when I do a wrong thing, *you* know how to fix it. You make me feel strong, instead of useless. Because you, for some reason I'll never understand, think *I'm* stronger than you."

"Maybe not physically, but every other way." You grunted, narrowing your eyes on mine, "How many times do I have t'tell you not t'call yourself *useless*?"

"Many more, probably." I kissed your chin, again rising onto my toes to make my face more level with yours. "You make me feel pretty. No one else does. You love me, every part of me, and see me in a way no one else can."

You kissed the tip of my nose, making my smile grow, "W'both know you're not jus' beautiful t'me... why I taught y'self-defense."

"Maybe. But, you're the only one who makes me *feel* that way."

That divine, lovely smile grew to showcase one of your perfect canines, "You're the only one who makes me feel a'lot of ways."

"Better be." I softly kissed your cheek, my smile somehow growing: as the stubble across your skin prickled at my lips in its oddly pleasant way. "Because you're truly all of me, my Love, and I'll *never* want anyone else."

"Never's a'long time, m'dear."

"Mhm. A long time I'll only spend with you, if you let me." I found your lips softly, briefly. "But, are you sure *you* only want me?"

You grunted, "Undoubtedly."

"Good." I kissed you again, quickly, getting that perfect smile to cross your face in its full glory. Speaking softly against your lips, as my hands slid down to find your either breast, "Then, how 'bout you kiss me back already, hm?"

You were about to do just that: about to start where we had left off before, now that you successfully made me forget about being in a rush. But, once again, our private world was broken into by that loud quake of thunder rolling through the woods, from the storm we'd nearly forgotten.

It cut through the silence from seemingly nowhere, making you pull away from me suddenly. Your bright, sparkling eyes wide and alert, scanning the trees as though that thunder would come and personally attack us. My own didn't leave you, but of course they rarely do: knowing I don't have to be aware of anything else, when *you* are.

A flash of lightning bathed the world in white light the moment after, revealing the dense, dark clouds of the storm above. Your gaze returning to mine as its new crack of thunder quickly rolled toward us. One side of your lips rising, when you saw the grin still over my own: simply there at the sight of *you*. "What did y'say about time?"

"That we'll have all the time in the world, if we get wherever you planned to hide from the storm?" Your smile quirked higher, as I rose back onto my toes to kiss your chin, "Where to, then?"

You grunted, "Quarter mile West. Know a cabin there."

"Until after the rain?"

"Yeah, then I've a'feeling you'll be wanting t'find your sister."

"Mhm." I lifted my hand from your chest to brush some of your hair behind an ear, out of your eyes, letting a goofy smile recross my lips. "Perfect."

You quirked a brow, "What?"

"Hm?" I quirked my own, "What, what?"

"Y'know what, m'heart."

"Oh... *that*." I let my fingertips feather softly over your lips, getting your brow to quirk higher, your lips doing the same. "You're just perfect, is all."

"Far from it." You spoke against my finger, making my smile grow. "And I, unlike *you*, have a'long line a'witnesses t'confirm it."

"Perfect to *me*. I don't care what anyone *else* says."

"Fair enough." You hardly moved your lips, kissing my thumb just before I could take it away: that perfect smile crossing your face as I ran my fingertips through your hair, pulling it back out from behind your ear to hang in front of your eyes.

A bigger smile lit up my face, too, the smile you would do absolutely anything for, "Perfect in *every* way, by the way, my Love."

"Right. S'long as y'know you're beyond perfect t'me, too, yeah?" You were about to lean back down and meet my lips with your own when the sky flashed with another strike of lightning, taking your eyes away from mine.

Up to the quickly darkening sky.

"I do, sweet Darling." My hand returned to the side of your face, turning yours back down to my own. I rose onto my toes to let my lips meet yours, to do what you'd been unable to. Kissing you in that brief, but sweet—as you say—way I usually do, staying on my toes as I pulled just far enough away to meet your eyes.

To see the many emotions, the thousands of thoughts, swirling in your irises.

Until you let your lips softly, slowly, come back to meet my own. A deep kiss that poured all of your love into me, because we both knew what was about to come along with the storm: and, it was just as you drew away, that the sky finally chose to open up over us. The deluge of rain descending from the sky, as the quickening wind slammed into us with a gust strong enough to slam my body even tighter into yours, to make even you stumble back a few steps before you caught us.

Strong enough to nearly make Silence lose his footing at the edge of the creak, the stones slipping beneath his hooves.

Your arm tightened around my waist, as mine did the same to you —holding myself as close to you as I could possibly be: knowing I wouldn't be able to stand against that wind on my own—your free hand snapping up to catch the horse's reigns before the wind could send him running. Releasing the reigns as soon as you were sure the horse wouldn't bolt, to yank a blanket—a plaid of many greens, mixed with various browns and blue—from within a saddle bag, to throw over my shoulders. Attempting to guard me against the cold, when we were otherwise defenseless: as the wind cut through our clothes just as easily as the rain instantly soaked through them.

Knowing the wool, somehow, would repel both water and cold.

You barely had time to wrap it around me, your arm covering my shoulders to hold me securely against you, before the brightest strike of lightning broke through the sky, creating the loudest thunder we'd ever heard. Something that made my eyes peek out from under your arms. Lifting up to see the trail of light remaining in the pitch-black sky, as the Earth trembled beneath us. My eyes swimming with worry: knowing the cause as if it were a logical answer to the question.

You felt my body tense, my hold on you tighten, and hunched even further over me. Your throat, right over my head, sending your voice rolling through me just like the thunder rolling over the Earth, "S'alright, don't have far t'go, baby."

"Get us there, okay?" My voice shook, shifting in your arms to be able to look up at you, "I'll come back to you."

"Yeah." Your lips found mine, fast but deeply, your eyes looking into mine with the vow that couldn't be broken. Asking it of me. "Y'better."

Both our eyes snapped up to the sky as another lightning fell, calling me: a single word left my lips, barely audibly, as I felt my body starting to lose sense. Losing all of the consciousness it had clung to before, starting to go limp in your arms.

It was the only word I ever needed to say: your perfect name.

The world was weightless. Light. A world without time and space, where she could be alone. *Free.* In the quiet, calm existence that comes when you're not yet asleep and not quite awake: the in-between.

A world where she could lose herself in the state of simply *being*.

Floating in a peaceful sea until she heard the howl of agony surging through the very depths of the world to find *her*, seeking the help only she could give. Until what she had been waiting for started to happen: until, the waves of water crashed around her. She didn't fight the pull of the current as she sank quickly lower, accepting where the Earth wanted to take her, what it wanted her to see.

Sinking until she let her eyes *blink*, and reopened them to the fast images playing in the darkness of the water. Photos snapping quickly before her eyes as if someone were holding a stack of them, shuffling through slow enough to see each frame, but yet not quite slow enough to see it entirely.

Showing my sister everything.

Now, since I'm unable to share exactly what she saw in the movement of the water, I'll take this moment to tell you more about her story. Since, I *do* have permission to freely share it here. I'll begin when things shifted from what was normal, *good*, to a life full of fear, anxiety, and depression: when she had stepped into the dark tunnel she couldn't find a light at the end of, no matter how far ahead she looked.

Because, when her body first started to rebel against her, fear lead her into a private world to face a horrible war she couldn't win, not alone. That she didn't yet know *how* to win, because she'd convinced herself it was better to hide her secret, rather than ask for help, since she thought it meant something was wrong with her.

That it was something no one would believe, or trust.

Now, we all know every girl on the face of the planet has a period, that's a simple fact: that time of the month when her body rids itself of its previous cycle to begin anew. Just like the moon. A cycle that should be beautiful, even with the discomfort it may bring. But, hers wasn't normal, it never had been: from the very first it had been never-ending, something she couldn't stop or find control of, which brought an agony that often went on for over a month with a crippling intensity that kept her from living her life. That made her truly *miss* life.

Miss everything.

It only grew worse as she aged, and was unbearable by the time she turned sixteen. An age where the world is meant to be at the brightest, the most free, where you are supposed to find your path and have the courage to follow it. But, for her it was a time when she only knew that pain, as the fire burning in her stomach raged so cruelly that even the thought of food became repulsive.

As the flame of *life* started to burn out.

I know it's far from a pretty thing to talk about, but these problems made my poor sister vomit at *least* weekly from the pain her body put her through, until it made her start to lose strength, and her weight dropped down to a low forty-something pounds. Because, all that scared girl knew, was that the lower her weight fell the less her body hated her: that the less of her there was, the less her body bled.

And, in turn, the more *free* she felt.

She didn't realize the lower that scale dipped the less of *herself* she had, until it was too late. Until she didn't know where she was, or who she was, only that the pain was less. But, by then, she was deathly afraid of asking for help, of admitting she needed it: which lead her to start feeling a sort of hate towards those of us who tried to help her. Hating us, because she knew she was lying *to* herself, and was afraid to recognize the truth behind it—how it made her truly hate *herself*, not us.

It wasn't until she was seventeen that she finally realized she wasn't alone, and that maybe someone *did* understand. It happened two months before the dream came, and had likely been the reason it did. When, well... when *I* reached out to her, knowing something was wrong beyond her failing weight. Seeing the anger, the hate, within her eyes and knowing the true cause wasn't those she blamed.

When I saw how she, herself, was almost lost.

I saw her letting herself truly fade away *inside*, into the dark nothingness where she couldn't feel pain: it was a time when she wanted to die, thinking there'd be peace on the other side, that there finally wouldn't be any more agony. And, she almost succeeded... but I found a way to pull her out.

It came in the form of an email, sent to her at one forty-one in the morning, October sixteenth. It was when she learned that I'll never give up on her, that I wouldn't let her end a life she's meant to live. It came the night after I had a premonition, the dreams that come before I wake, after *you're* already awake.

The dreams that make me "psychic."

I didn't tell her what the dream was, that it happened, until years later. But, it's one of the most terrifying I've ever had—like *yours*. One that made my world stop, and become focused on saving my sister's precious life. It'd started in an elaborate church, beautifully lit up in a kaleidoscope of colors as the sun broke through the stained-glass windows. I'd been walking up its aisle, arm-in-arm with you, up to where a priest and my family were gathered around something. And, from the beginning, I knew the air was too heavy, too thick... far too *wrong*.

We walked slowly, my arm only slipping from yours to catch your hand as I pushed through the crowd to see what they were looking at. To see the beautiful cherry-wood coffin waiting there, covered in brightly colored daisies. And, as I studied it, Katie had come up to my side, a peaceful smile across her beautiful lips... and, even before she spoke, I knew I was the only one who could see her.

That my sister was showing herself to me, as a *spirit*.

She spoke calmly, as if her words were a perfectly fine thing to say, stepping closer to me and resting a hand softly on my shoulder. Something my sister would never do, avoiding contact as much as we do, except in a situation as serious as this. She'd said, softly, and to me alone, "I'm going to die. Soon. Unless you stop me… But, I *want* to die. Please, Danie, just *let* me die."

I'd woken from the dream terrified, spending that day looking for some way to help her, to regain her trust. To open her up to the idea that life isn't bad, that she's *loved*. And, to prove to her that losing her would absolutely destroy me: since, she says, I'm the only one who she truly cares for.

That night, as I said, at one forty-one in the morning, I sent her the email. A simple email with a poem I'd found for her inside. It was one of few days in the darkness she remembered: the day she woke from the nightmare. And, she has saved the email, and has read it more often that I ever thought she would, because it *saved* her life.

She's always said, after that day, that *I* had.

And, it was the day she started to regain her lost strength, to remember who she is: at the lowest point she had lacked the strength to stand, her muscles leaving her body with her weight, but *that* day she started to get back all she'd once lost. It was a slow process, one she's still fighting, but a fight she then knew *she* had the power to win.

Just as I always knew she could.

After, as you know, I started to tell her about our dreams. Trying to show she wasn't the only one who had to hide a big part of herself, for fear of the world thinking her insane, or exaggerating. Then, we started to share dreams, as I've mentioned, and she truly *did* make it her sole purpose to help us. It really was a light in her darkness, until time started to pass and—to her eyes—her plans seemed useless. When what she tried seemed to lead us further apart, instead of closer. And, she began to feel it's her fault we weren't together yet, because I was worried about helping her first.

Because, she knew I'd never leave *her* until she could stand alone.

So, that was when she started to figure out what road she's meant to follow, but it took a while to find *her* destined path. You see, at first, she tried to live like a normal human being: tried working a few jobs, but quickly realized the thought of working a newly re-found life away felt like signing up for voluntary jail—something you, and I, both undoubtedly agree with—which was a fate she wanted to avoid at all cost.

To avoid being trapped again… her biggest fear.

She tried to go out on a date, too, to open her world up to the thought of love as she saw how happy it made me, even if I "just felt it in dreams." She thought it was what normal people do, and all she wanted was to feel "normal" again. But, she didn't last a single date before she learned it wasn't for her, learning the true path ahead of her is one of independence, not with another person: that being alone isn't bad so long as it's the right *kind* of alone, the kind that brings her happiness, and strength, not fear.

And so, she eventually realized she's not *just* a normal human being, and couldn't pretend to be anything except as she is. Because, she's meant for much more than she could've ever imagined back then, than most could ever imagine even now.

She's made to be one with *life*, as she is with nothing else.

And, it was only once her strength started to return that she began to get a grip, at least mentally, of her monthly agony. Facing it with the knowledge that one day she *would* be able to get it under control, once she was ready to do what she knew she'd have to. It took a few years more, but that day came when she fell into a different sort of fear that made her want *life* as nothing else could. When fear became a stubborn determination to survive, and she found herself ready to finally face all of her fears, and to finally be free of pain.

Now, since there really isn't a simple or easy way to say it, I will just say it bluntly: at the young age of twenty-five, my beautiful sister had to have a hysterectomy.

She finally found out just how hurt that part of her body was inside. That it honestly *had* been trying to tear her apart from the inside out all that time, that her instincts had been right, and she never should have doubted herself. And, once she finally learned the way to fix it, and why it *was*, she hadn't hesitated.

So, really, at the age of nearly twenty-six... she set herself free.

And, she woke from that agony to see the true dream of where she wants to be: the dream of seeing the world through the lens of a camera, marking down every moment of her freed life through videos and images. Knowing her true purpose in this life is to help others any way she can; that by sharing all the struggles she's faced, she can save someone who's going through the same or similar. And, although she's spent so much of her life being afraid of living, she's now finding the way forward.

Finally finding her road, finding freedom.

But, she still had that *one* thing to do before she took hold of her true, and destined future, or else we knew neither of us would ever let the other go. So, when I stole a glimpse into her mind within that calm water, I felt her promise at the forefront of her mind: she wouldn't let anyone, or anything, stop her from doing what she had to do. *Nothing* could stop her from setting the one she loves the most free.

Because, my brave sister... she truly knew *everything*.

She burst free of the water just as a flash of lightning tore through the darkness. Her bare feet stepping onto the lake's rocky shore as the ground shook beneath her: letting the heavy rain pounding against her body turn right to steam when it touched her skin. Her gaze, and focus, set on the figure moving through the dark shadows of the woods before her, appearing as one with the leaves as they swayed in the brutal wind.

She closed her eyes to focus on sound, hearing its heavy hooves clomping against the slick leaves and dirt as it slowly came nearer to her, just as she did the same for it. Hearing the horse let out one heavy snort, as she opened her eyes to make out its dark silhouette through the trees, as she eased up to its side. Taking small, soundless steps, until its black eyes and ears tilted toward her, releasing a snort as she slowly lifted her hands to show she didn't mean any harm. As the horse, its jet-black hair glistening from the rain, stamped a hoof solidly against the leaf-covered ground to say it knew she wasn't a threat, and neither was it one.

A horse that I *definitely* recognized, from her dreams of before.

Her hand softly patted the horse's strong throat, a smile finding its way across her lips as she carefully slipped her foot into its stirrup, swinging onto its back as another flash of lightning lit up the dark sky.

Her heels clicking against its stomach to urge it forward, as the thunder rumbled. Sending the horse galloping into the woods, as her grin grew wider, because she knew nothing would be able to stop her, not now: from the moment she fell asleep, and the image of a door flashed before her eyes, she had known that life, hers *and* ours, was finally going the right way.

That it would be from there on out, if she did what she had to.

She urged the horse to go faster, its hooves beating in time with the thunder. Setting her sights on the shadow of a tall mountain looming ahead of her as another strike lit up the sky. A laugh leaving her, "Let's go, Thunder, huh? To the sea!"

Because, you see, she said it was thanks to me that she had learned how to love, by learning how to love and *protect* me. And, she thought the only way to return that favor was to follow the road ahead, and to make sure *we* followed the right road, too: because, she finally knew how to get *us* to find our love in the waking reality.

She laughed again, yelling, "We're going to be free!"

Because, my sister... as I said, she knew *everything*.

Silence ran at that magic speed where you're moving so fast it's almost like you're flying instead of riding a horse at all—I came back as another bright strike lit up the sky, its loud crack of thunder making me flinch into consciousness.

Making your hold tighten on me, your thumb tenderly rubbing against my shoulder to say you were there, too. Holding me securely in front of you, hunched over me with the now equally soaking wet blanket wrapped over all of me up to my eyebrows, to keep the wind from touching me. Your voice muffled, "Y'with me?"

I only managed to grunt, but that was all I needed to do. Peeking out from under the blanket to see what was coming up ahead of us: the faint outline of a cabin etched into the darkness, barely in sight yet standing like a welcoming beacon in the storm.

An unassuming safe haven.

Silence brought us safely into its stable as my eyes found the sight: in through the double-doors that had been left open as if expecting someone to need inside quickly, such as during a storm. Cutting off the roaring winds of the storm, the pounding of its heavy rain, so much that it would have seemed nonexistent if its tin roof didn't softly ring with the drops, if the open and swinging doors didn't let an eerie moan creak the walls under the strain of the gusts.

I only had a second to glance around the place, able to see how the stable was clean and maintained with room to hold likely ten horses. Before you dismounted, leaving the horse free to settle from the run as it chose, with me securely cradled against your chest. Keeping me surrounded by as much of your warmth as possible, in a way that made me realize how much I was shivering, uncontrollably, from the cold of that rain and wind: from being empty of energy after being both pulled to my sister's mind, and helping you. Noticing how you shook, too, even as you tried to hide it.

I nestled closer, to share my heat just as much as I stole yours.

"Y-you're sure n-no one's h-here?" I looked up at you from under the blanket. For a flash of a second seeing myself through your eyes:

just how fragile I appeared. As you shifted my weight to hold me fully with your forearms, rather than your hands, letting you briskly rub wherever you could reach in an attempt to warm me. Even when we both knew it was impossible just then, when we were covered by wet clothes and in a cold, drafty stable.

You started toward the open doors as you did, your steps slow and short from your clingy clothes and cold joints. Yet, still stubbornly trying to deny you were just as cold as me. "We're 'bout t'find out, m'light."

You stepped back into the storm, keeping our bodies tightly together to fight against the cold, against the force of wind that tried to sway your path. That made *me* bury my face into your safe chest at the first piercing gust, but *you* hunch further around me to cover as much of me as you possibly could. Sacrificing yourself, as you always do, as you pushed against the wind, fighting across the distance between that stable and the cabin. Only finding the slightest relief once we reached the tiny awning over its door, that barely blocked the rain from our heads, but seemed like a godsend.

Truly, my Love, your determination never ceases to amaze me.

The home was abandoned, as you knew it would be, but it never even entered your mind to knock. As soon as we made it beneath the awning you turned your body to the side, making sure none of me went passed you, as you slammed your shoulder against that door to shove it open in one solid hit.

Easily snapping a chain that had been locked into a latch.

You carried me straight to where a small couch hid in the darkness, steps from the door you'd kicked shut behind us with your foot. A couch that was smaller than even a love-seat yet spanned most of the room's width, covered in a rough animal hide which matched the one on the floors, with a low wooden coffee table in front of it and a chair placed by the door, set barely out of its path: filling the tiny room to the brim.

A small stone fireplace was in front of that table, cleaner than used fireplaces have a right to be, free of any soot or residue. You went there next, once you had sufficiently made sure I was alright, to find the wood neatly stacked beside it. I watched, curled in a tight ball with my knees hugging my chest, as you threw several logs into the hearth, slipping your knife free as you knelt before it.

Watching, openly fascinated, as you arranged the logs just as you needed them to be. As you sliced your blade just once down the metal of a fire-poker-stick-thing—I'm *sure* that's the technical name—creating a spark that easily set the tinder, and then the logs, ablaze. And, I didn't even try to hide the amazement in my eyes when you turned back to me, making a smile cross your lips as you rose back to your full height.

Returning the knife to where it belonged, as you softly cleared your throat, "I'll go see 'bout finding you a'dry blanket. Get outta the wet things. Alright?"

"A-alright." My smile grew enough to push up my cheeks, letting you see it existed even passed the blanket. Which made *your* smile rise enough to showcase that canine. "That'd be g-good."

"And, *you*," You closed the distance between us, stepping over the table to kneel in front of me and kiss my forehead, the only part of me in your sight. Making my eyes close as your beautifully hot breath blew over my skin, "Will stay right *here*."

"Mhm... *Right* here." I smiled up at you. Seeing that smile quirk higher, as you rose and then crossed the distance to what I assumed was a kitchen. A room just out of my sight: taking *you* out of my sight, so it was only then that my eyes slightly explored.

Seeing how a few feet off to my side the wall had two narrow doors, side by side. I could assume one was a bedroom and the other a bathroom, but I can't confirm either. And, just beyond the fireplace was the equally narrow arch leading to the kitchen, that you had taken, and which I later observed shared the fireplace on the other side.

I didn't have time to see much more before you came back, in less than a minute, carrying three neatly folded blankets on your one forearm, balanced so you wouldn't get them wet against your body. And, in the other, a plate of chocolate chip cookies.

A small thing that made a smile come back across my face.

You followed my eyes to the sight as you came to where I was, moving slowly with that carefully balanced tower of blankets. Lifting that plate higher, a smile returning to your face: quite proud of yourself. "Figured y'wouldn't mind."

"I *never* mind those." I let the blanket fall down to my hips just so you could see the wide smile across my face as I sat up. By then, the perfect little fire had already warmed the room to a pleasant degree, taking the chill away from the air. "They were just waiting for you, I suppose?"

"Of course." You set the plate on the table, tugging the wet blanket from over me to throw it carelessly somewhere by the archway: I heard the wet-slap as it landed on the floors. As you leant close to me, as if it were a secret, "By *magic*."

A laugh left me, making your eyes shine with that pride as you draped a dry blanket just so over me, wrapping another over the first before I knew you grabbed it. Tucking it around me more thoroughly than you had to, taking your sweet time. Letting a smile cross your lips as my brow quirked in question of your thoroughness: as another laugh happily left me, and once again made you very proud of yourself.

You quirked your own brow, mirroring me, "Good?"

"Mm." I looked down at my blanket cocoon, another laugh leaving me, "I think you covered all the bases, yeah."

"Good." You threw the last carelessly over your bare shoulders as you sat beside me, wrapping your arms immediately around *my* shoulders to pull me safely into your side. Letting your hands resume the brisk rubbing on my arm, the one not against you, and on that same side's thigh: really, any part of me you could find.

I, of course, leant into you the moment you offered your warmth. Burying my face into your chest, where it blessedly wasn't hidden by your carelessly placed blanket, letting all of me curl against you. Even letting my boot-covered feet slip underneath the blankets as my legs bent closer to yours.

Having you catch the underside of my knees when I did, drawing my legs over yours to wrap me in part of your blanket, too, both to share your heat and mine. Pulling the zippers of my boots, running down the backs of my calves, slowly down to my ankles once my legs *were* over yours. Slower than you had to, but truly just as perfectly slow as I wanted you to, letting your warm fingertips skim the skin that had been hidden beneath. Before slipping both free of my feet, and letting them drop heavily down to the floor, somewhere.

My eyes fell closed as you did, basking in your heat.

A happy moan leaving me as your strong hand found my feet, rubbing warmth into both of them in turn. Until, I felt you nudge the top of my head with your chin, asking me to look up at you; and, I did the moment you asked, when you leant slightly back to see me: how I was shivering significantly less than before.

A sight that let you lean right back down to me, tenderly kissing my forehead. And, keeping your perfect lips soft against my skin, to let your warm breath flow over me, "You're alright."

That goofy smile crossed my face, "I'm with you, aren't I?"

"Yeah." You kissed me again, "Definitely with me." You nodded for me to return to your chest, and again I did so without hesitating, letting you rest your face on the top of my head as a deep breath ran through you. Quiet for many slow breaths, with your voice barely audible when you did speak again: calm as we only are when alone, and together. "Didn't think I'd actually enjoy the storm."

"Mm?" I kissed your chest, your heart, "I knew we would."

"Yeah?"

"Mhm… Had a feeling everything would be fine."

"Yeah." You kissed the top of my head, nuzzling with your perfect nose in a way that made a smile quirk back over my lips. As your hand, the one that'd loved my feet, found my back to slowly rub over me in smooth gentle circles, in the way you know always has the power to calm all of me: by then, all my shaking had died away, as had your own. "Guess I had a'feeling, too."

The cabin fell into a perfect sort of quiet: with the hum of rain on the roof, the slow creaking of windows in the wind, and the occasional roll of thunder shaking under us. Creating a moment of gentle peace, where we could simply just *be*.

We stayed simply so, in silence. Until, I lifted my face from the beautiful warmth of your chest in search of the eyes that always know how to say more than any amount of words ever could. Your perfect, beautiful eyes that were then heavy, relaxed, just as content as my own; letting your lips quirk lazily upward as I met those eyes, sharing a thousand words in a single glance.

Creating a vision I could admire all my life, and never tire of.

But, my eyes hesitantly left yours after that wordless conversation, to see where the untouched plate had been forgotten. Letting a heavier breath run through my lungs as I drew my bottom lip between my teeth, my eyes lifting back up to yours. Debating if I wanted it badly enough to leave your magnificent warmth, even for a short second, in order to reach it.

And, deciding that was something I absolutely didn't want to do.

Your smile twitched slightly higher, changing the decision for me, as your hand left my back to slowly skim its way up my calves. To find the under-side of my knees, and ease my legs from over yours. I released my lip to put a pout over my face as you did, but still shifted the rest of the way from your chest. Leaning on the low backrest, instead, to let you lean forward and drag the plate over the table, into your reach.

Causing a horrible sound that made you glance at me with a perfectly exaggerated cringe as you created it, drawing a laugh from my lips. But, you already know by now that everything you do is perfect to me.

"For *you*, m'lady." You placed it on my lap with a quick wink, that smile lifting to expose a perfect canine as you did: that little wink you do which is *truly* too skilled, I'll add, since I was unable to deny the wave of vibrant heat it made rush to where you knew it would, making me forget any memory of the cold, of anything else.

Only aware of you… as I usually am.

You acted oblivious, rising to step over that table when you heard my sharp intake of breath, acting as if the strongly burning fire was now in sudden need of more wood. Grabbing two logs from beside the fireplace, and kneeling on one knee in front of it as you meticulously placed them inside. With your brows drawn forward, and your eyes set on that single task. With a look that I've seen across your face thousands of times: trying to decide between what you thought you should do, and what you wanted.

But, I knew better than to ask, knowing you'd rather show the answer on your own, when the time came for it. Instead, I clumsily wrestled an arm free to take one of the five cookies from the plate, a smile coming over my lips when I heard a heavy breath of air leave you.

Your quiet laugh, hearing me struggle for freedom from your cocoon.

I took a small bite at first, timidly testing if I would taste it at all in the dream. I did, finding it soft and perfect, but of course it was: it *was* something created by the magic of your mind just to ease the stress of everything else going on.

And, the worry to what you didn't yet want to say.

By the time you were satisfied with how those logs were placed in the bright fire, I had nearly finished that cookie. My eyes studying the flames as they flicked up higher, stronger than before. Burning far more than we'd technically needed it to, turning the room from mostly warm, to verging on *too* hot.

But, that wasn't the point behind you tending it then.

You stepped back over the table, sitting on the edge of the couch beside me. With an amused smirk across your lips, as you fixed where the blanket had fallen from one of my shoulders in the struggle. Handing me another cookie from the plate once you had, to save me from fighting free and losing that blanket again.

I talked around it, as I wouldn't comfortably do around anyone else. But, again, I think you know by now: I'm only truly comfortable with you, it's always as simple as that. "Thank you, sir."

"Gladly, m'lady." Your lips lifted to expose that canine, leaning back to where you had been before. Letting your arm rise to wrap around me as soon as I started to nestle back into your side, my smile wide across my lips. You kissed the top of my head, as I tucked it beneath your chin, a content sigh leaving me. "Y'really *do* amaze me."

Again, I talked around it, "What way?"

"*Every* way." Your hand slid further over my shoulder to find the side of my face, brushing my hair behind an ear as I plucked a third cookie from the plate. As your free hand reached to do the same, talking around it just as I had to mine. "But, y'did scare m'half to death."

"You, too." I kissed your knuckles, on the hand still feathering its way softly across my face, before I took that hand into my own. Tilting my head onto your shoulder, to meet your eyes, as I kissed your hand in the soft space between thumb and forefinger, more tenderly than such a thing should be able to be. "Sure you're okay?"

"I am." Your smile grew when I gently turned that hand to kiss the sensitive inside of your wrist, my fingers tightly entwining with yours. I didn't need words to show all I said in doing so, we rarely do. Making you clear your throat as you snatched the last cookie, trying to ignore how my kiss had almost undone you: but, the poor cookie was already gone before you could even finish speaking. "Thanks t'you."

A small smile crossed my lips, "To us, you mean?"

"Sure. But, mostly you." You lifted our joined hands to rest two fingers beneath my chin, gently lifting it up higher. Letting your lips find mine softly, sweetly but briefly, keeping your forehead against mine as you pulled away, to ask, "Y'tired, m'dear?"

To most that would probably seem like a strange thing *to* ask, considering we were already "asleep," in a sense. But, we tend to feel tired just before we're stolen away from a dream—and even more so when we wake, usually—as some part of our minds or spirit runs out of the energy to keep us present, and where we want to be. So, to us, it isn't strange at all.

I shook my head, a wide, likely goofy smile crossing my face. That *one*, which you would do anything to create, "Feel like I've been sleeping for days."

"Even after... what happened?"

"Thanks to your '*magic*,'" Silly as it is, the cookies helped my energy return to me: that's why you'd created it. "I'm not leaving this dream until you do."

"Right, then," Your fingertips feathered over my chin, "I'll never leave."

"Even if that means dealing with... everything else?"

"Even so." You closed the small distance between us, kissing me beautifully slowly, tenderly. With *that* magnificent smile crinkling around your perfect eyes as you pulled away. "Jus' not right now, yeah?"

A smile returned to my lips, too: you never are subtle, no matter how you may try to be. "Well, the storm's likely keeping the world a bit busy right now..."

You grunted, "Hopefully."

"And, it would most likely stop us from going anywhere, if we tried *to* deal with anything *right* now... wouldn't you say?"

"Considering," Your fingers again gently lifted my chin to be closer to yours, letting your lips feather over my own in that way you have which might as well be kissing me still. "I've other things on m'mind t'get in the way a'success? Yeah... I'd say."

I quirked a brow, "You've *things* on your mind?"

You grunted, "Bit distracted, yeah."

I blinked my eyes slowly, innocently, "By?"

"Many things, related t'*one* thing."

"Oh?" My brows furrowed, as though confused, "What one

thing?"

"Can show you... *if* y'want m'to." Your glittering eyes told me, had there been any doubt before: but, there certainly hadn't been. "Just ask."

"That's *all* I have to do? *Ask?*"

You grunted, "And, I know how much you *do* like asking things."

"Hm, I do... But, that's a hard thing to decide."

"Y'have all the time in the world."

I again quirked a brow, "*Do* I?"

"You *do.*" You kissed me, slowly and sweetly, those eyes staying with mine. Just as those lips didn't leave my own, "Would wait eternity for *you.*"

"Hm..."

You quirked a brow, "Hm?"

"Just thinking."

That silent laugh left you, "Yeah?"

"Mhm."

"And?"

"Well, I *might* want you to show me, after all." My eyes flicked down to see your lips passed your nose, slowly lifting back up to yours. "I mean, if you *really* want to."

You grunted, "I do."

"You can think about it." I tilted my face slightly away when you went to kiss me, making an impatient grunt leave you. A sound that drew a laugh from me, just as you knew it would. "You know, if *you* aren't sure—"

"Jus' because I *would* wait an eternity, m'heart, doesn't mean I *want* to." You tilted my face up further, your hand this time keeping me there in case I may try to delay more. Letting you take full possession of my mouth in the matter of a moment, your deft tongue easily parting my lips to find my own: a kiss that showcased just how insanely much a man can possibly love a woman.

Something my mind never can seem to truly grasp the extent of.

Your free hand tenderly found my thigh as that kiss deepened, drawing a soft moan from me as you shoved my skirt out of the way to find my bare skin. Your fingertips applying just the perfect amount of pressure to make my hips instinctively shift closer to you. To make that magnificent fire spiral through my veins. As I shifted to give you all the permission you needed, to do anything you wanted.

Going wherever and however you wanted me.

Your hand traveling slowly, lovingly, tenderly higher up my thigh as you let your kiss progressively become more aggressive, more passionate. As both combined made every last part of me respond to you: as the sacred place just between my legs spoke in need of you, in want of you. Your touch pausing just shy of my hips, breaking away from that kiss to once more meet my eyes, our heavy breaths merging as one.

"M'Danie—" Your words fell away, utterly forgotten, when I pushed the plate out of my lap—we both heard it shatter, but obviously, didn't care—letting my hands find your either shoulder, to steady my balance, as I brought a leg over your lap to straddle you. Having your perfect hands find my hips to keep me there, caressing me, as my lips made your head tip back: slowly, tenderly trailing kisses down your throat, down over your clavicle, before gliding back up to find your lips. Only drawing away as you shoved my skirts further out of your way, meeting your eyes as your hands lovingly found my behind, drawing me closer to you.

As close as we could be, with your jeans still in our way.

You kissed from my lips slowly down to my jawline, freezing when my hand glided lower down your chest, down passed your stomach. Those beautiful eyes finding my own as I easily slipped the buckle of your belt loose, and set both button and zipper hidden behind it free. Making your breaths hitch when my hand found *you*. Watching, my eyes lost in the depths of yours, as your perfect eyes reacted to my touch. Making your hips instinctively rise: the deep rumble vibrating through your throat telling me I was doing just the right thing.

What I hoped to do.

I kissed you, once but slowly, before pulling back away, my eyes staying on yours. How you watched me, in blatant awe, as my free hand pushed the blankets away from my shoulders, letting my fingertips find the bow of my dress. Your eyes following as I slipped the second crossing of the ribbon free, followed by the third, parting the fabric to just between my breasts. Revealing how fast they rose and fell in search of breaths I can never find, not when your perfect eyes watch me *that* way: in the magnificent way that tells me I truly *am* your entire world.

A way that made me stop there, slowly bringing my hand down to find one of yours at my hips, gently lifting it to let you undo the rest. Letting you slip the ribbon free, the fabric falling down to puddle around my hips as your gentle hand found the soft, bare skin hidden beneath. Drawing me closer to you, as your hand's perfect warmth sent a pleasant shiver through absolutely all of me. Kissing you, as those magnificent hands tenderly explored all of me, freely as only you can, or ever will: letting me take full possession of your mouth as you did the same to me, entrusting all of myself to you as you did the very same for me.

Entrusting each other with everything we are.

"Love you." It left my lips between heavy breaths, my hands finding either side of your perfect face. Letting me see the most beautiful sight in my entire world: the sight of *You,* my one and only Love.

That smile returned to your lips, laying your perfect nose against my own; your lips feathering mine in *that* way as your body started to, at first, move gently with mine. Making sure I was entirely alright, watching me as your pure, divine love possessed all of me. As your magnificent body truly became one with mine: as the same perfect feeling possessed all of you.

You spoke between heavy breaths, too, "Love *you*... More than anything."

And, just as you always do, my sweet magnificent Love, you showed me just how much one *can* be loved. Sweetly. Kindly. Patiently. Drawing me into the world where only we can ever exist—lifting us high into the beautiful stars glistening somewhere through the storm above us. Into that perfect world of love few can ever *truly* know: the rare state where two can be one not only in their bodies, but their spirits and their minds, surrounded by sweet, incomparable love.

Because, you... well, you truly *are* my everything.

And so, we stayed surrounded by one another's love, as united as two can possibly be, never parting for more than a few breaths before we became one again: explicitly one another's in every way possible.

Until that storm started to quiet into a distant hum…

I mentioned before that we have always known what we are to one another, but if I had to name an exact time when I discovered what true love *really* is, I'd say it had been when I was still only four, but close to five. Which, I know, most would say is too young for a mind to understand *any* sort of love, much less grasp the difference of *true* love. But, well… I wasn't a normal little girl, was I?

I was a little girl who was free to know *herself*.

Now before, I've only just touched on how much my family supported me, as I am. So, I'll take another moment here, to say more. Because, if it wasn't for them, I truly wouldn't be here now, would I? And, they certainly do deserve a word of appreciation, when I know just *how* lucky I am… when I know how differently it went for you, and how much cruelty you faced because of it.

"Mirroring" my life as the *opposite*, as I wish you hadn't had to endure.

But, as those close to you started to title you as insane—at the age *most* parents do try to talk their child out of believing the usually unseen, but you were too stubborn and brave to deny it—I was lucky enough to have parents who always listened to what I said, no matter how strange my words may have been: who didn't only just *listen* to my words, but *believed* in me... who never once made me think something was *wrong* with me, never tried to change who I am, or tell me to ignore how I was.

Who let me feel loved, for being who I am.

My perfect mom even made sure I had an hour or two alone every day, just to be with you, instead of trying to tell me you didn't exist. *Trusting* me. Because, as she's said to me, she knew you were more than just "imagined" even then, and didn't want me to doubt myself, to deny being who and as I am.

Because, my beautiful mother *always* believed me, more than anyone.

Even when other parents gave her crap for it, she always stood up for me—far too many times and ways to name, but it *always* meant the world to me—whenever other kids, or even parents, tried to make fun of me or tell me I was crazy... she, much like your mother, told me to just ignore those who tried to change my mind: that they may never see the world like I do, but that doesn't mean *my* eyes see it wrong.

We just see life... *differently*, you and I.

She's always known that, my patient mother. And, she was always willing to listen if I woke from a nightmare and went for her help, no matter how late or how often I needed her. *Hearing* every word I said, and never discouraging me by saying I was just a silly child making things up for fun: *she* believed when she saw how much *I* did, that was all she ever needed. Talking to me about my dreams, and also about you, as though it were a common part of life for everyone, giving me the courage to trust myself... to believe in myself, as she believed in me.

She'll never know how much that means to me.

And, my perfect father wasn't any different: even if some things I have said in my life were beyond his comprehension—and, he's never all too fond of hearing me talk of *you*, for protective fatherly reasons—he never discouraged me from being myself, or said I was wrong just because he doesn't see things in the same way. He's always done his best to understand me, listening and trusting in all I say, trying as he can to see things as I do, even if he can't quite grasp it for himself... No matter what, I've always known my father will *always* be standing at my side, supporting me.

Because, nothing I do will ever stop them from loving me.

Honestly, they have been so unspeakably patient and kind when it comes to the side effects of being as I am, that I cannot even begin to thank them properly: I wouldn't have been able to take the time, and the chance, to truly be as I am *meant* to be if my mama hadn't listened to me, or if my daddy hadn't worked so hard to make this life as safe as possible, and give me the freedom to *be* free as myself.

So, believe me when I say it—even if I know every last child out there who's had a happy childhood says so—because I really do mean it: they truly *are* the best parents out there, the best ever.

Putting up with *me* should be as much evidence as one needs to believe it's so.

That was how by the day of this memory, nearing five years old, I was more sure of my mind than most are at that age—than most even in their much later years: how I could already grasp those things that some will never be able to, such as true love.

By simply trusting what I *knew* was felt.

It was one of those days of many as a child that stand out clearly. Because, as I said, it's the day I began to realize you're far more than just a close friend. Back then, I'd lived in that small home, in Florida. In a town that had once been perfect in its simplicity, before it grew into a bigger town just like any other. Our home had been perfect, too, to me. Small, simple, and perfect. With a family who, of course, was just as perfect as the rest of the world had been—though, if you ask me they still are—and as far as I was concerned *you* were a part of that family.

Because, well, you *are*.

Back then, my parents hadn't been rich by any means, rather quite the opposite. Yet, they had somehow made sure both me and my sister wanted for nothing. We had been practically raised in parks and our local library, free things that taught and gave us far more than most anything else could. Things that gave me ample time to let my mind run free… run with you. There was the beach, too, of course. We spent a lot of time on the soft, white sands. Happy memories that likely lead to the *many* future dreams I'd spend with you when my life changed for the worse years later.

Because, you've always been close to the beach, too, just a far different one.

At the time of the memory we're slowly getting to, my father's parents were both still alive, living just a few miles from where we did. We'd visited them nearly every day, and that was likely what was about to happen that day. We were probably going to see them later, waiting for my dad to come home from work, when it happened.

But, of course, we'll never know how true that is. I'm not afraid to say I can never be sure of any detail about the scenes beyond those where you're involved: you know that you always carry a brighter beacon in my memory than anything else, a vibrant spotlight I can't ever imagine forgetting even if I had to. But, I suppose, the whys and hows and whats around the memory don't relate to the story right now anyway, so let's say what I *think* was going to happen was likely true, since it's what usually did.

Now, I'm relatively sure it happened sometime in the Summer, since I know it was the extravagant hot outside that most Florida Summers were. And, when I was a little girl, from the time my parents pushed me on the swings until we moved away from that little home when I was nine, I would spend hours and hours a day swinging on the set my dad had built for me and Katie.

The best swing-set ever built, so far as I was concerned.

So, that day hadn't been any different: after breakfast I skipped right out to those swings. Truly, I *did* skip, as you know. Wearing my favorite dress and the big blue bow I always had in my hair, holding it out of my face. Even at the time, I had known it would be a day to remember, and made a point to wear my favorite things because of it. Because I'd woken from our dream that morning realizing just how you affected me compared to everyone else: how the vibrant happiness you bring was a thousand times more than any other I experienced; how I felt differently towards you, *with* you, than anyone else.

I should pause a moment to explain how, at that age, I could only "talk" to you if I was alone: and, if I didn't get that time-alone, as my mom will tell you if you ask her, I couldn't focus on anything else. Frustrated that you could be waiting, and I wouldn't be there for you. Truly, if I didn't get to talk to you, be with you, I was quite a bear to be around, to deal with. They were the only times mom said I was ornery as a child. But, either playing alone in my room for a few hours a day, or swinging let me find you: they were my ways of meditation, back then.

And, that day was no different.

I had rushed through breakfast and quickly gotten dressed to go out and be alone on my swing before Katie could do the same and ask me to play: to do something which I couldn't find *you* by doing. Staring out at the tall grass in the vacant field behind our home, at how it swayed in the gentle but hot wind similarly to how the other field did in dreams, until I heard the swing next to me squeak under your weight. A weight that shouldn't have been felt, but somehow was.

That always proved you were more than an *ordinary* spirit.

A wide smile crossed my face when I heard it, my eyes instantly finding you: a grin that vanished when I saw how you were cradling an arm in your lap with the other's hand, as the hurt arm's hand fiddled idly with the swing's chain. When I was a child, as I am to this day, at least to you, I'd been very blunt. So, I'd said what I saw before I could stop the words from leaving, "You're sad."

My bare feet skidded clumsily against the worn-dirt beneath me, stopping the swing suddenly. Sudden enough that the dirt bunched in my toes. Leaning close to you, with concern openly across my face: thankfully, if my mom had glanced out just then, she and everyone I knew was used to me talking to myself, and doing strange things... so, no one would've questioned me.

You didn't answer, but you rarely did: it was when I saw you "older," in dreams, that you truly spoke to me. So, your silence didn't faze me in the slightest, I simply leant closer as if closing the space would solve the mystery. Holding my brows tightly together, studying you, "You're hurt?"

"No." You jerked your hand quickly away from that hurt arm, angry at yourself for showing pain, as your own brows tightened into a furrow. Just as they still do, when you're thinking or concentrating: or, frustrated. Your sad eyes softening only to ease the worry in my own, as you also still do. "Y'were gonna say something. B'fore."

That gave me freedom to say the many things I'd indeed wanted to say, and I didn't hesitate to prattle on too fast for most to follow, just as you knew I would. Letting you and I theorize about feelings: a long discussion that took longer than it would have between any other two kids. Because, I did most of the talking... and once I start to speak, there's no stopping me: as *this* "letter" for you proves.

My sparkling eyes—everyone always said just how *much* they sparkled—studied your face for any words you wouldn't say, as I still do: like you're the finest and the most fascinating thing anyone can ever see. Because, well, you *are*. "You know how a princess is to a prince instead of a friend?"

"Sure." You shrugged a shoulder, "Why?"

"You're like a prince, to me. I think."

"M'not a'prince."

"Okay." I'd resumed swinging, only speaking as I swept by you.

"A *knight*, then." I swung by. "You protect me," —swing— "from all the bad things." —swing— "And, call me" —swing— "a princess."

"Don't do a'good job at it... protecting."

"You *do*."

"If y'say so."

"Mhm. 'Cause it *is* so. So, will you?" I looked at you with my eyes wide, as if I had really thought you would say "no" to me. "Be my knight, I mean?"

"Sure. If y'really want me t'be."

"I do."

"Alright." You stood, suddenly, stepping right in front of me. I skidded to another stop, barely not "hitting" you. A wide grin across my face that perfectly matched the one across your own. "I swear t'always protect you, best I can, as m'princess."

"Always?"

"S'long as y'let me."

"So..." I laughed: your favorite sound in the world, isn't it? "*Always?*"

"Yeah." You brushed stray strands of my messy, frizzy hair behind an ear, resting your hand on my small shoulder as you leant timidly towards me to softly kiss my cheek. In the way that without fail creates my goofy grin. "Always."

My mom had called me in for lunch as another giggle left me. And, I'd reluctantly left you to go, since I didn't yet know how to keep our link going without full focus. But, it was only a couple hours later that I made it back into solitude.

You'd been "there" waiting long before I stepped into my

bedroom, following as I skipped to the desk in the corner, where my favorite play-toy was. My *favorite* toy was a plush *Eeyore* on my bed: as if I knew even then that your spirit animal is, well, a donkey. On the desk was my toy of a princess's castle: the real version of which I had grown up in just as much as that beach, which was why I used princesses as my idea of love. A toy castle that was likely smaller than I remember, but had been giant to me, big enough to take up almost the entire surface of that desk.

I played for a while in silence, with you simply watching, until you gently swept my hair behind an ear to better see my face. In a way that brought my eyes right to you, to where you knelt beside me.

You shifted closer, saying, "Tell me?"

I looked at you as though you knew the answer to everything, because in my world, you *do*. "There're different *types* of love, right?"

"I guess, yeah."

"And, I love *you*. But, not like a brother. Or a friend."

You laughed, that breath of air, "Hope it's not like a'brother. That'd be... strange."

"So... it *is* like mama? And daddy? *Love, love?*"

You tilted your head, those brows furrowing as you thought my question through, entirely. Your eyes truly sparkling like the sea under the sun on a bright morning when they returned to me, a small smile across your lips. "Yeah. I think. It's love, love."

"Okay." My own smile returned as you brushed that stray hair back again. I turned in my seat to face you, my eyes sparkling just the same for you: since, you're the only one and thing they ever truly sparkle for. "Then, that makes sense."

And, it did, that simply.

A simple, short moment—though I likely told it in a rambling way—that had been the start of knowing just how much I'm in love with my knight… and *only* you.

True *love, love.*

We ended up on the cabin's floor, beside the fireplace—which was possible, since you'd shoved the table out of the way—laying in perfect stillness. Our breaths flowing calmly, in unison, creating the only soft sound in the otherwise silence.

I rested with my body entirely on top of yours, the furs from the couch pulled up to my chin: chilled, as both our bodies glistened with sweat and the fire faded. Resting an ear over your steady, perfect heart, with one of my arms curled around the front of my waist to find yours over my ribs—our fingers securely entwined—and the other over *your* waist, over your ribcage on the opposite side as my body; with your free hand resting heavily on my back, its arm laying over mine across your chest. And, my legs wrapped around yours, my feet against your knees.

Truly, as close as possible.

A deeper breath ran through my lungs, my face nestling against your warm chest. A smile crossing my tender lips at the feeling of you all around me, at the undoubtedly real soreness of my body: at the signs it hadn't been *just* a dream, but part of reality.

As impossible as our reality may be, to most.

My eyes blinked slowly open, and heavily. Having to squint against the bright sun streaming in thin beams through the boards of the shutters, its light falling right over my eyes as I slowly tilted my face up to find yours. My smile lifting higher when I found you almost dozing, your face peaceful and relaxed in a way that made you look younger than you usually do when you're aware, alert.

Peaceful as you only are with me, and I with you.

Your beautiful head rested on a pillow found on the room's chair, tilted down from leaning your chin against the top of mine. Letting me study you openly, freely, which I certainly did. Watching how your perfect lips stayed so slightly parted to deepen your calm breaths: showing the tips of your front teeth as you gently pulled your bottom lip between those teeth when you inhaled, the nostrils of your perfect nose subtly flaring as you exhaled. How your brows twitched every once and a while as you thought, a small movement that only happens if you're otherwise still, unable to be so entirely. How your eyes shifted beneath their lids, your dark lashes forming perfect half moons over your perfect cheeks; your mussed hair falling completely over your forehead, and most of those eyes, hanging down to brush across those cheekbones.

Making you truly look angelic.

I brought my hand away from your waist to gently brush some of that soft hair from your face, tucking it behind one of your ears: a gentle touch that made a breath push free of your lungs with enough force to ruffle *my* hair. Both your hands tightening on me as your beautiful eyes blinked heavily open, showing you had been deeper in sleep than I thought. Letting a sleepily lazy smile cross your lips at the sight of me.

When you found you were back in *this* dream.

"Hey." Your voice was hoarse, husky, making my grin somehow grow, as you lifted your hand from my back to brush the hair out of my face: mimicking what I had just done to you. That perfect smile of yours lifting higher, in a way that made my heart do those strange things beneath my breasts, as another deeper breath ran slowly through you. As your knuckles feathered over my cheekbone, "Somehow, even prettier than a'second ago... keeps happening t'you."

"Hm, was just going to tell you the same." My hand gently flattened on your breast, helping me ease higher up towards you. High enough that my tender lips could meet yours, briefly and sweetly. Kissing from your lips down to your chin, speaking against you. "I love you, my Everything."

"Hm... was jus' going t'tell y'the same." Your smile grew to expose those canines when a laugh left me. Your head tipping back, against that pillow, as my lips feathered across your jawline, trailing down your throat. Letting your hand tangle in my hair, to cradle the back of my head: encouraging me to keep doing exactly what I was doing, as my lips trailed over your collar-bone.

I kissed my way down your chest slowly, deftly, my tongue skimming your skin as I crossed over one of your breasts. Lifting my eyes up to yours as I found your nipple, getting a soft groan to rumble deep in your chest, those eyes falling closed: telling me I was accomplishing what I set out to do. Skimming my hand slowly down from your breast, over your abdomen, about to venture lower when your fingers tenderly started to massage the back of my throat to bring my eyes back to yours, gently drawing my face back up to yours. I went the moment you asked, my hand skimming back up your chest to find your shoulder, rising closer to you.

And, you kept me there without saying a word… and I patiently waited, until you finally began to say what had been on your mind all night. What you, my Love, had wanted, and *needed*, to say for a very long while. What had made you fall into my arms, back at the quarry, "I never told you… what happened."

My voice was barely audible, "You didn't have to."

"But, I *want* you t'hear, now." You released a heavier breath, drawing me close to kiss my forehead, and staying there. Letting your beautiful voice be partially muffled by me, while avoiding my eyes. "For some reason thought I could hide it from you, so y'wouldn't be disappointed."

"You know I'll never be disappointed, not by you."

"Well," You grunted, "Y'don't know what a'piece of shit I've been."

"I do." My hand slid over your chest, over your heart, "You weren't."

"Yeah, I was." Your arm slid partway from around my waist to rest its hand over the small of my back: your fingertips tracing my spine and the curve of my behind as you spoke. "You remember when I tried to run from… my life, and that shit happened when I was… mostly homeless, for a'while… and, more desperate than I should've been… and, it lead me t'do things I shouldn't've?"

I let my nose nudge under your chin, "I do."

"Will always remember when I told you… and y'said—"

"'I can live without a penny in my pocket, but not without you.'" I slowly drew my forehead away from your lips, to let *my* lips kiss your jawline. Finding your eyes, as a not quite even breath left you. "I still mean that, my Love."

"I know…" You kissed just beside my lips, speaking against me as your gentle hand skimmed all the way up my spine from my behind, to the nape of my neck and slowly back down: in a way that made my eyes fall softly closed, despite your words, "I've tried to get my shit together since then, when I realized y'were seeing it, too. Seeing *me*. And, what y'had t'think of me." You grunted, "But, still failed you, didn't I?"

I nudged your nose this time, with mine, "You've never failed me, Love."

"But, I *did*, baby." Your hand paused where it was on my behind, its fingers gently caressing me, "Knowingly fucking myself up worse, as I *tried* to get m'shit together… I call that failing you."

"But, you *know* that wasn't your fault." I opened my eyes to find yours, to show how much I *did* know. One of my hands finding the side of your face, to show how much your every sacrifice means to me. How much *you* mean to me, my Love. "No matter what anyone's said or done to you… no matter *who* tried to say you're insane, or how they hurt you when… no, sweet baby, that wasn't your fault."

"But, now…" You released a heavy breath. The hand in my hair gently bringing my face back to yours, our noses side by side: staying silent with our breaths for another little while, before you very quietly asked, "How long have y'known the truth t'where I am, my light?"

"Ever since it's been the truth, my knight."

"And, y'still don't want to run away? You know I—"

"Shush… you're the kindest, most sane, *good* soul in the entire world." I kissed your cheek, making *that* smile start to appear. "No matter what may try to stop me, I'm going to find you, set you free, and never let you go." I drew enough away to kiss your nose, "I'll *never* run from you, my Love. One day, you'll realize that."

You kissed my forehead, "You're far too kind to me, y'know that?"

"There's no such thing as being 'too kind' when you hold more love in your pinkie finger than most hold in all their hearts." I again kissed just to the side of your perfect lips, "So… how about you maybe consider letting me help you put some of that 'shit' back together, hm?"

"Don't worry, that." Your lips twitched fully into that magnificent smile, "Soon, you'll get t'help put plenty a'shit together, my Life."

You stole my lips before I could say more, kissing me longer and much deeper than I'd expected. Pulling a content moan from my throat as my body drew tighter against yours, wanting to be as close to you as I could possibly be.

Even closer than we already were.

You shifted me onto my back. Pulling away from that perfect, divine kiss hesitantly, briefly, meeting my eyes as you eased back into me: into the sacred haven made only for you. Catching my lips as a sharp, content gasp escaped me, my hips instinctively rising to meet yours, moving with you. Speaking against my lips, in *that* way, "Love you, too… by the way, m'heart."

You carried me back up to the beautiful stars, into our magnificent world of divine love, slowly and passionately, magnificently—perfectly.

And, we only returned to the Earth when we *absolutely* had to.

It was probably another hour before you rose to peek through those shutters, to see if the long gone storm had truly cleared: knowing it had, but hoping it hadn't.

Leaving me to freely watch as you found and tugged your jeans into place, on your way to that window. As you leant a hand heavily onto its frame, and squinted to see through, letting your hair hang in front of your face to conceal all but the tip of your nose; letting me admire the beautiful image you made, utterly mesmerized by just how absolutely perfect you are.

Because, it's truly impossible *not* to admire the sight.

I studied, openly, as you left that window and bent down to retrieve my dress from the floor, to place it in my waiting hand. My eyes watching, unashamedly, how your muscles moved in response to what you were doing: in the way that truly seems like magic. A sight I could truly stare at for eternity, and never ever tire of. Watching, as you pulled a new T-shirt over your torso—which you'd found under my dress thanks to unexplainable dream-magic, this one black rather than gray—acting oblivious, so I wouldn't turn shy and stop: you didn't even care that it went on crooked, twisted, too busy trying to ignore me to realize it was, forcing your mind to focus on hunting down the blade that'd rolled across the room when your jeans had fallen.

Finding it beneath the chair.

By the time you returned it to your waistband I'd pulled my dress back over me. A sight that made *you* lose all train of thought, all breath, when you turned and found my back. When all you had been fighting to avoid by keeping your eyes away almost won anyway—you stood still as a statue, I was very aware, watching as I got it in place.

Which was likely a good thing: had you moved, we would have never left.

I only turned to face you after I tied that bow, fully dressed except for my boots. My eyes almost timidly lifting to yours, feeling my cheeks catch fire at the awe across your face. At the thoughts clear in your mind. I lightly cleared my throat to bring your gaze up to mine, away from my body.

Again, otherwise we never would have left.

"S'it okay?" My voice was barely audible, shy, my hand lifting to pull some of my hair into my sight, to twist its ends almost nervously around my fingers. I meant, by the question, if it was in *place*: for instance, if said hair was a disaster. But, you looked at me as if I had just spoken an unknown language.

You quirked a brow, waving one of your hands in my direction to indicate all of me, slowly closing the small distance between us, "Y'can't be serious."

"Quite... is it?"

"Yeah. It's 'okay.'" *That* smile crossed your face, the one I'd do absolutely anything to create; the one that always makes one cross my own in return, "You're only a'Goddess."

My hands rose to find your either breast when you stopped in front of me, flattening my palms over the soft fabric covering you, "You look pretty okay, too."

"Yeah?"

"Yeah." I shifted closer when your hands found my hips, asking me to do just that. My smile growing wider as I gently pushed against your chest, as you tried to come even closer. Making a small pout cross your face, which also made a laugh leave me. "We should—"

You interrupted by leaning down, unhindered by my hold on your chest, to let your lips find my own. Kissing me, slow and deep. Your hands drawing my hips closer as your tongue easily parted my lips, taking full possession of me as though it were both the first and the last time you'd ever be able to. Making a soft moan escape me, my hands tightening around that incredibly soft fabric covering you, urging you further down to me even when I knew we should have been preparing to leave.

Because, we'd never spend a single second apart if we didn't *have* to.

I pulled away from you reluctantly, kissing several more times before I was able to stop. Walking over to sit on the edge of the couch before you could protest it. Though, you weren't tempted to, only letting a smirk cross your lips: amused by my stubborn decision, and how I started tugging my boots on my feet as we spoke just to keep from coming back. "I assume you heard, from my head, that she's going to the sea?"

"Yeah." You rested an elbow on the fireplace's mantle, appearing relaxed even as you only did so to keep yourself from resuming what I'd interrupted. I knew, you see, by how your other hand shoved into your hair, pushing it out of your face simply to do something *other* than what you wanted. "Was planning on taking the pass 'tween the mountains… Probably right where the fire is, by now."

I quirked a brow, tugging up a boot's zipper, "It survived the rain?"

"Yeah." You always refuse to admit *how* you can know these things: that you feel everything that effects our world, because you're the one who gives our land *life*. As much a part of the Earth as the trees and soil. "Don't worry, that. We'll manage."

"I'm more worried about why it's still here, Love." Because, you *are* one with this Earth, and it always reflects *you*. I rose to come back to you, placing my hand tenderly over yours, on the mantle. "But, I *do* trust you."

"Yeah…" You turned your hand under mine to entwine our fingers, squeezing my hand in a way that spoke a million words, "I just hope I won't let you down."

"You—" I never got further: a sharp gasp taking my words as my hand instinctively tightened around yours, to a likely painful degree— clinging to you as the lifeline, as the tether, you truly are for me—as my *sight* suddenly snapped away from what my eyes were seeing, to see a flash of the woods just outside. The dense black fog rushing straight for the cabin, for us. Coming back to you before the gasp entirely left me, as I fell limply into you and you safely caught me: as my eyes blinked back to yours, with blatant fear across my face. A fear that told you what was about to happen long before I truly *told* you, in a barely audible quiver, "It's happening again."

The world fell apart before my words had time to fade, when the darkness tore that perfect, safe, little cabin to shreds around us.

It started with a roar... an unexplainable sound, but the closest that I can come would be saying it's surely near what one hears as a tornado plows through their life, yet of countless voices lost in a desperate screech of agony, rather than a powerful spiral of wind. Cloaking the world in their smoke, as the shadows crashed into our haven, breaking through the shuttered windows and tearing apart the walls surrounding us.

Destroying absolutely everything they touched.

You'd reacted right after I spoke, diving onto that pushed aside coffee table as the world turned dark. Landing on your back with my body clutched to yours: your hand catching its side, tipping it over with you to protect your back with its meager cover. By the time they started to break through the windows you had me securely pinned to a wall, covering me unflinchingly even as the table behind you gave way, and those shadows reached *you*... until, even you couldn't stop them from tearing you away from me; when they *all* swarmed us, and threw you as far from me as they could.

To get rid of you, any *way* they could.

And, their hands were already on me—tearing at my dress and breaking the skin beneath, trying to rip *through* my skin to find my spirit—before I even heard the crash of something breaking: before you fell onto whatever that was. Pulling me back down when I tried to use the wall to rise—to find you, when I heard your voice bellowing for me through their screams—throwing me hard enough to once again make my head crack on the floor after my body, making stars dance before my already blinded eyes.

You yelled my name as they threw me, this time more breathlessly, as you tried to fight off those holding you back: you never *do* lose sight of me, even when you can't see anything else. And I, somehow, found my hands and knees before the stars could even leave my eyes, desperately trying to see through the haze of black smoke to find you: smoke that was already making my eyes sting and water, taking away what little vision I'd had. Having to feel blindly along the boards beneath me with my hands to find my way in the darkness; not even aware the floor was covered in sharp shards of wood, cutting into my palms and knees, until much later when I remembered how to feel anything other than the need to reach you.

Not even truly aware of the shadows constantly catching at my ankles, until I had to kick them off of me. Irritating me more than anything, since there was only one thought in my mind.

I made it to the fireplace by the time I heard you again. My ears filtering through the cacophony of screams to easily hear the roar of *your* voice: a bellow that spoke all the fear and frustration I felt, too; that let me finally find *just* enough energy to reach you. I didn't even know that I had slid up the wall beside that fireplace, as you made that roar, until I was standing on my wobbly feet and leaning on the mantle; didn't realize how the shadows were falling away from me, how I was glowing so brightly that the whole room was vibrantly in sight—the smoke turning into a more misty, clear haze—until my eyes found *you*. Standing at the center of a ring of spirits, fighting them so fiercely that I can only compare you to an enraged bear. Just as I didn't realize I had cried out your name, until I was already suddenly safe and in your arms, with my face buried into the crook of your shoulder, and my arms wrapped tightly around your neck.

Just how on Earth you managed to shove bodily through the countless shadows trying to stop you, by any means, I'll never know. I just know that my enraged bear suddenly had me in safe arms, and that in the same heartbeat—as soon as I became weightless in said arms—you were slamming a shoulder through what was left of a wall, freeing us to the outside world. And then, in the next heartbeat, somehow Silence was with us, and you were lifting me onto his back... honestly, I couldn't make sense of anything that happened after the shadows crashed into the cabin, until I felt the undeniable cry of agony that shot through you as you *did* lift me, even as *you* didn't feel it.

You were far too high on adrenaline to feel *any* pain.

I only caught a glimpse of your face as you mounted in front of me—which you only do when you want to quickly leave someplace, and need the freedom to make the horse do so—but the glimpse was enough to see how your eyes were reddened, their delicate blood vessels broken; your nose dripping blood, with the skin at its bridge split open; your lips equally split, sending blood down your swelling chin; with your cheekbone gashed and leaking crimson, too, already purpling with a deep bruise. And, I definitely *felt*, how your stomach was severely swelling from likely broken ribs.

But, beyond all that, which I knew we'd fix as soon as possible, all I knew was that you were *alright*: and that meant absolutely everything to me. Even if I *was* very, very mindful of your ribs when I wound my arms around your waist, the moment you were seated. Resting my chin on your shoulder, my voice barely audible, "Love?"

You grunted, "Yeah?"

"I *love* you, my Everything. You know that, don't you?"

"Yeah." That magnificent smile crossed your perfect lips: making all that happened a moment ago seem okay. "Yeah, my Life. I know."

The sky was a dark hazy gray from smoke, but not yet from a fire.

What was left of the woods around the cabin were yet green, their old trees standing tall, alive. But, I saw, in the only glance I spared for the world behind us, how rapidly the forest was vanishing under the assault of those cruel shadows, stealing down to the very essence of the trees, the warmth and heart they carried. Turning the green forest into a sea of black and grays, ravaged by the shadow's desperation for life, until those strong trees looked as though even the slightest touch would turn them to ashes in the wind: as many had, judging by the heavy density of the air already.

It was only then that I learned *how* the forest was withering, as you'd said. And, the sight not only hurt my heart, but filled all of me with an undeniable sense of guilt… because, even if I knew it would all be worth it, by the end, I also knew what was still coming, before: and, how it would be faced, mostly, because of and *for* me.

No matter what that meant for yourself.

Of course, I know you will say I had nothing to feel guilty about, because you had made the decision on your own, and were prepared for what would follow. But, I also knew *why* you set it free, and why on that specific night: what had lead you to make the choice, that allowed the darkness to find its way back into our world—how it had been set free, purposely, by a decision to end the suffering of the past, to *face* the fears instead of hide it deep beneath the soil, so it would never be able to control you again. And, while it's partly true that none of the destruction or pain faced that night would have happened if you hadn't set it free, if you hadn't asked them to step out of the shadows and into the light, we both know it was something that *had* to happen for us to finally stop holding back from being who we have always been meant to be. So, I will say it, too: you had absolutely nothing to feel guilty for, either.

Because, we're equal in all things… even causes to events.

But, that didn't mean that I could stand the thought of looking back at the withering forest, again. Keeping my eyes, forcibly, facing forward: peering over your shoulder, instead, to see the fire approaching us. A sight that was mildly less concerning, since I knew the plan spiraling quickly through your mind, for me to see: explaining how it existed not to get in *our* way, but to keep something trapped inside the Earth, for us to find on our own terms, instead of it finding us unawares.

I released a heavy breath, speaking at the volume no one else would be able to hear, but you always do… the fact that I spoke right beside your ear simply made hearing my words easier, "Can I ask you something?"

"Anything." You grunted, "Always. Y'know that."

"Even if I already know the answer, and why you won't want to say it?"

"Go ahead." Your hand, that had been resting on your thigh, found my own at your waist to entwine our fingers, to say it was alright. Making another grunt, one of worry, when you felt the splinters in my palm that I hadn't even realized were there, and how quite a few of them weren't exactly dainty in size. You were already starting to gently pluck them free one by one before you grunted again, "S'your other hand the same?"

"Probably... I don't know." I couldn't help the small smile that crossed my lips when you brought my hand up to *your* lips, pulling a more stubborn shard out from below my thumb with your teeth. Resting my chin on your shoulder, both to let you see more of me if you were to want to, and me see more of you. "Was more concerned by your broken bones than a tiny splinter in my hand."

"*Ribs.*" You grunted, "S'nothing."

"Ribs are bones, last I checked." I let my finger flick the tip of your nose after you used the teeth technique again. Getting a smile to quirk over your lips, before I slipped my hand free of yours in an attempt to say it wasn't a big deal: but you instantly took the other, to say otherwise. Making a theatrical sigh leave me, "Stubborn man."

"I am." You kissed my palm, "Your question?"

I tilted my head closer to yours. Kissing the side of your throat and keeping my lips on you as I spoke, in that way you've taught me: the continual kiss. "How long has it been? Since you opened the quarry."

You grunted, speaking almost inaudibly, "Few weeks."

"Why, Love?"

"Same reason I changed m'mind about taking the road." The pass safely between the mountains, you meant... but, I'd known since before the shadows that we wouldn't. I was just afraid of what would follow. You brought my hand back to your lips, tenderly kissing the center of my palm, "M'not going to let anything hurt you again."

"Or *you*, you mean."

"Yeah." You lowered our hands—mine, by then, entirely splinter free—down to rest on your thigh, tilting your head to let your face rest alongside my own. "That's what I mean, my Life."

"So..." I turned my face to meet your eyes, and you did the same to let me. "You mean, get rid of them completely?"

"Completely, m'light." Your hand squeezed mine, the silent words spoken deep in your perfect eyes getting my smile to grow into its likely goofy state: because, I knew that it was true, that it was possible. "Yeah, that's exactly what I mean."

And, we both knew what *that* meant.

Traveling the rest of the way to the fire in silence: carried only by the steady thump of hooves against the Earth. But, even had we wanted to continue speaking—aloud, at least, our minds never really *do* stop talking, do they?—by the time we'd drawn near enough to truly see the fire, the poor air quality had made me bury my face into your throat, just as you lifted your shirt to cover your nose and mouth. Fighting against the air, as well as how the fine layer of sweat covering us let the ashes rising from beneath the horse's hooves stick to our damp skin. Dust that stung harshly at our eyes, having to squint to stay open at all, fighting to see the ruined world around us; to keep your gaze on the peaks of the mountains, reaching above the trees, to keep us on track.

Because, you *always* somehow know the way.

We'd been riding for over an hour when I let my eyes peek from the cover of you. Instantly starting to water and redden from the air as yours were, blurring nearly to a point of being blind. I broke the silence, then: my voice muffled from hiding against you, making you turn your face toward mine to hear what I said, but slight enough that your eyes didn't leave the mountains. "How much further?"

"Not very." Your voice was hoarse from the dry air, and muffled from the shirt over your face. But, of course, I had no trouble hearing you. Feeling your hand tighten on mine—reassuring, in a way no one else has the power to be, for me—as you tilted a shoulder closer to me, higher to block my face from the cruel air. And, as you nodded down to me, "Hide your face, for me. Don't want your eyes hurting, m'dear."

I narrowed my already squinted eyes on yours, "What about yours?"

"Mine are used t'being abused." You winked, since I could at least see *that* part of your face. "Cover your eyes, my light. Won't see you hurting again."

"But—"

"For *me*, baby." You softened those eyes in a way that told me you'd put a pout over your face. Making a humph leave me, since I couldn't ignore that. "Please?"

"Fine." I nestled my face against you. Kissing your throat at the tender point just beneath your ear, making a chill run slowly up your spine. "I'll just blindly admire my husband's magnificence... and how he's undoubtedly the strongest being ever."

"Would argue," Your thumb swept tenderly over my knuckles, "But, we've already been through that, m'light."

My eyes fell calmly closed, "Have we?"

"And, agreed you're far stronger than I'll ever be."

"Hm…" My voice was barely audible, completely muffled by you. But, I again spoke right beside your ear. "I don't think that's how it went."

"M'certain it was."

"Hm… Well, you *do* have a memory that far surpasses mine." My nose nuzzled against you, stopping you from protesting *that* fact by agreeing to the previous subject. "So, if you say so, I'll believe it."

"Yeah." You drew your shirt away from your face as you lifted our joined hands up to kiss my knuckles. Confirming you certainly *did* say so, in a way that made a goofy smile cross my face. "I do."

I opened my fingers from around yours to feather over your chin as you kissed me again, my grin growing as I felt your beard scratch at the pad of my fingertip. At how I felt a smile quirk over your lips, too, "I love you, my stubborn, beautiful husband."

"D'you?"

"Mhm. Just a little bit." My smile somehow grew, "A teeny, *tiny* bit."

"Hm… Well, I," You kissed my hand again, paying extra attention to the ring on my finger. "May love y'back, my stubborn, beautiful wife."

"Oh?"

"Yeah." You kissed my fingertip as it feathered over your lips, drawing a soft laugh from me when you gently bit its tip. "Jus' a'wee bit, m'life."

We let that love carry us, in a mutual state of silence, until you drew the horse to a stop where the flames were no longer at a distance, but flicking up at the forest around us. Your squinted eyes tightening to see through the haze, the flames, to see where we needed to go: letting me see through your eyes, to keep me from opening my own.

Letting me see how the path ahead was lit up by the bright, scalding oranges, reds and blacks of that fire, twisting up the trees to ignite the canopies up above. Turning the remaining air stiflingly hot and ashen, to the point that you wouldn't have been able to breathe if your face hadn't been covered as it was, and only barely able to at that. But, after just a moment of pause, you urged the horse back into motion, easing as close to the flames as we could be without being *in* them.

So close, that boiling heat became the only feeling in the world.

Yet, the brave horse didn't complain, taking us far closer to the fire than instincts should have willed it to go: trusting you, as I do, since you never give a reason not to. Even when Silence's entire body was glistening with sweat—as yours was—panting since he didn't have the luxury of covering his face, fighting for each breath… the good horse stayed by the flames, not ten feet away, as your squinted, burning eyes scanned the face of the mountain through that fire, hunting for what you sought.

I kept my face hidden, until you cleared your throat.

Tilting your face toward mine, to meet my eyes once they were free, as you drew Silence slowly to a halt. Letting me see how your beautiful face was by then completely covered by soot and ashes, by the sweat that turned both to mud. Your eyes looking brighter against the angered red the whites of those eyes had turned to, from the sting of the burning air. From how the veins had been broken *before* the fire touched them. Your hair dripping with sweat so heavily it looked black rather than its natural color.

Of course, I should add, *my* face was still clean thanks to you, from how protected I'd been, and I was somehow only slightly perspiring: but I didn't notice either, until I took note of how wet your torso was beneath my arms, your back the same beneath my body and face. Showing just what you had endured, to protect me.

You spoke when our eyes met, your voice extremely hoarse. "Bag t'the left."

I found what you wanted shoved on top of everything else in the saddlebag, pulling two of the many canteens out as you yanked the blanket—that same woolen one—out from the other bag. I handed them to you, securely latching both bags closed before I returned to the safety of you, my arms wrapping back around your waist.

"Legs. Over me." You threw the blanket over us the moment I did, covering all you could with its fabric: able to cover all of me once I had my legs crossed over your lap, leaving your boots and half your calves in sight. Barely leaving enough of the horse's face exposed to ensure he'd be able to see. Dumping the water over that wool in hopes the fire would take longer to catch with its barrier, even if it repelled most of it.

My voice was now almost comically muffled, "We're going *through* the fire?"

"Yeah." Your hand found my ankles to keep them securely in your lap, to ensure none of the fire would be able to reach me if it tried. "Jus' hold on t'me, m'dear."

I did, of course… and very tightly, as you sent that brave horse galloping into those flames, your body hunched low to cover your face with the blanket: running for the opening in the mountain you'd spied, with a level of trust few horses would possess.

But, then again, I suppose it *is*, mostly, a dream horse.

We were immersed in those flames for just seconds before that brave dream-horse broke through and entered the mouth of the cave. Only seconds, and yet still far long enough to feel like eternity: having the thick wool catch fire the instant we were in the fire, burning quickly through to try and find us, but not fast enough to truly find where we hid before we were free of the flames. Though, enough—even when your boots and the horse's legs at least avoided the flames, from the width of the blanket, they didn't escape the heat—for the leather of your boots to slightly melt, and for Silence's fur to singe…

While I was entirely untouched, thanks to you.

You were off its back the moment we were within, throwing that burning fabric off us and into the flames to free us of its fire before my feet even dropped to the ground. A stone floor that blessedly held ankle deep, refreshingly cold water to cool your feet: water likely from the rain. Freeing the horse as soon as possible to let those burning hooves prance a few feet further inside, stomping them in the water to try and ease the suffering, while whinnying loud enough that it echoed through the tunnels beyond.

A sound that seemed even more hurt in its echo: that made my heart ache.

You stamped your boots against the ground, too, unknowingly mimicking the horse. Turning to find where I stood after taking a quick inventory of your own well-being, knowing I had been perfectly safe behind you. Your brows furrowing when you saw my body already faintly radiating with your light, "Y'alright?"

"Mhm... You?"

"Yeah." You nodded towards me, your brows furrowing even tighter. Thinking. "You're glowing. Not enough t'get through the caves, but... give me a'second."

I knew what you meant to do.

"Love..." You ignored me. Reaching back to pull the knife free of your waistband: my eyes studied your every move, hoping I was wrong but knowing I wasn't, as your left hand rose toward that blade. "Don't do what you're going to."

"W'only know two ways to—"

"I pick option two, then."

"Option two on its own isn't possible right now." That far too lovely smirk crossed your lips when I glared at you, "We've t'work with one and a'taste a'two."

"Love—"

You dragged the blade's sharp tip across the palm of your hand, not even cringing as it broke your skin: sending bright crimson instantly down to find the water, making my face pale. I *felt* it do so. You tucked it right back into your waistband once the slice was made, your eyes never leaving mine. "There, step one."

"You were *already hurt*, you dork." I slapped your chest. My hand catching the hem of your shirt, tugging it up to showcase the purple of the bruises from your broken ribs. The other waving at your hurt face, at what hid beneath the sweat and ashes. "I didn't *need* any *incentive*."

That smirk grew, "Y'could've reminded me of that, before."

"You gave me two seconds!"

"Did, didn't I?" You glanced at your hand as if you truly hadn't thought of it, when we both knew you had. When we also both knew it worked as you'd wanted: my aura was already brighter, desperate to help you. You shrugged, "Done now, anyway."

"Yeah. So, let me fix it, you beautiful dork." I caught that hand within both of mine. Examining the cut across your palm as your unhurt hand found the side of my face, to tilt my face up toward yours.

Your thumb finding the underside of my jawline, tilting it higher as you leant down to me. Near enough for the tip of your perfect nose to touch the tip of mine, as *that* smile quirked higher over your lips: making a matching smile cross my own before I fully knew you made it. "That's step two, my light."

"Seriously," A laugh left my lips, blowing my breath across our lips like gentle fire, making that smile quirk even higher. "You're *such* a dork."

"Sure am." Your magnificent smile crinkled your beautiful eyes, "And, I'm all yours, my Life… if you'll have me."

"Just *kiss* me, Love." I rose onto my toes, my lips finding yours as a laugh left you. Letting one of my hands catch ahold of your shoulder, drawing you a bit further down to my height as I rose higher onto my toes, and my other hand flattened gently across your hurt side. You grunted when I did, telling me just how hurt that side was, making me pull away far enough to meet your eyes, wordlessly asking if you were alright.

That smile came back to your lips, showcasing both canines and softly crinkling the skin around your glittering eyes. Creating what's truly the most beautiful sight in my world. "Thought y'told me to kiss you, my light."

"But, I hurt—"

You interrupted in the best way possible. Your lips finding mine when they'd been parted, your tongue easily finding my own. Kissing me deeply, passionately, intensely: in the only way you truly know how *to* interrupt me. Making my knees thoroughly give out beneath me, a happy moan rumbling through me as your hand, tingling as it healed from my light, found my waist to catch me. Pulling my body securely to yours, as the other hand tangled deep into my hair, tilting my face higher to let you kiss me deeper, until it was just *us* left in existence.

By the time you pulled away, that cave was filled by our own sun.

The caves had existed perhaps even before the rest of our world had come to, made from stories heard as a child of what may hide within the darkness of the Earth: tales of dark spirits hiding where light can't find them. Some parts of the world use stories of trolls or goblins to explain what lives there, just as others know them as shadows, or even demons. Because, whatever the name, humanity tends to fear what hides in the shadows they cannot see... because, they fear the shadows inside themselves.

And, all those stories—undeniably based upon some truths—had given your young mind an explanation for the cruelty in your waking life. Had let you create a secret place within our safe world, hidden far below the calm and beauty above, where you could release your hurt and fear.

Where you could let pain and sadness free.

Letting those caves become the home to your nightmares, just as the hallways held the darkness to me. And, that's how I knew what you were trying to hide as we nearly ran through the tunnels, your eyes set on the dark path ahead. Refusing to meet mine, when you knew I'd be able to see the emotions you didn't want to feel, much less show. And, *that's* why I didn't care about the fatigue clawing at me from within as the light drained my energy: my only thought and concern was to ensure nothing could get between us and the other side.

Between me, and you, my Everything.

We travelled through the tunnels without seeing any sign of life, or any movement, beyond the thick gray dust lifting beneath our fast steps. Everything eerily quiet, every sound seeming muffled and an echo at once: we didn't even have the sound of horse's hooves, having left him behind back at the beginning of the caves... since Silence wouldn't have been able to fit in the narrow tunnels.

But, you never once questioned which turn to take even as it separated into multiple paths, knowing the way as only you can. Making our progress fast, and sure. Until the tunnels lead us to a steep slope where the caves had at some point started to cave in. Though, perhaps "slope" isn't the right word: really, it was an incline of loose slabs of stone falling suddenly downward to make a crude stepping-stone ramp leading to the lower levels of the caves; a ramp with many blank spaces dropping into the darkness below, if one were to miss their footing.

And, who knows what one would find if they did so.

Here, we had to travel most of the way down nearly sitting, with me heavily relying on your steady balance instead of my own clumsy one—even still, I managed to slip into your back many times from that clumsiness. And, admittedly *jumped* onto your back in terror at one point, when loose stones suddenly shifted beneath me. Stones that had held in place blessedly long enough for your weight to pass to the next, but not for mine to do the same. Letting a few of them unkindly take the time to reveal the void below as they fell, showing what waited if we reacted too slowly: taking away what little confidence in my footing I'd had before.

So, yeah, if I'm honest… I went down clinging to your back.

And, when we made it to where the slope fell away to a sudden not at all terrifying end dropping the last ten feet down—a rough edge that dropped down to pitch-black-darkness below—you jumped down without a moment of discussion behind it, as the brave nut that you are, to test the landing.

To see what waited.

I stayed sitting precariously on the ledge up above, waiting to hear you land solidly on the hard stone somewhere below before I called down. Somehow, I was out of breath despite you carrying me most of the way, "How is it?"

"Dark. If *only* I knew someone—" You weren't able to finish the thought before I came crashing into you. I didn't do so on purpose, a yelp leaving my lips when my body became suddenly weightless: when, as the klutz I am, I slipped off the ledge as I leant forward to try and find you in the darkness.

But, well, *you* had likely expected that to happen.

My yelp turned into a laugh before it ever felt any sense of fear: I knew you'd catch me, with a warning or no. And, you did, catching me safely in your waiting arms, as mine looped loosely around your neck and shoulder. Not even pretending to offer letting me back down, keeping me right where I was—knowing how happy I am, to be held by you... because, you're just as happy *to* hold me, however long it's for—as our eyes took in the world around us.

A world of seemingly impossible peace, if you didn't know what had been trapped there: if we didn't know it was hidden *somewhere* with us, then.

The caverns were lit up by our light, casting magnificent shadows like hundreds of silhouettes dancing in the distance, swaying gracefully through the stalagmites as you turned to look around, shifting our light. A peaceful world extending miles around us in every direction, its ceiling rising what had to be at least thirty feet high above our heads with thousands of stalactites stretching down toward us: a ceiling that our light changed to appear as if the shadows were rippling waves, as if we were really beneath the sea not the Earth.

A silent, heavy world with absolutely still air, that would have probably been cold, if we hadn't been sharing our own warmth with one another. Surrounded by a feeling of being the only ones in existence—even when we knew we weren't—the only living things to *ever* exist. By a tranquility filled by the sound of our soft breaths, sounding like panting in the utter silence, and the distant sound of water dripping down from above, slowly creating more of the countless sculptures creating that world.

A work of art that would never stop growing, changing.

I was parting my lips to break that silence, my wonder-filled eyes coming back to yours, when our beautiful sense of peace was suddenly shattered by a deep, blatantly pained groan reverberating through the caverns.

One that seemed both miles away and right by our side at the same time.

You had me on my feet with you in front of me in the matter of a second, freeing your hands in case something planned on attacking us, protecting me from whatever that may be. Hearing the groan come again just a moment after the first, followed by something slowly dragging, heavily, against the loose stones of the ground. Sliding its way across the floor until a shard from one of the many stalagmites crunched under its weight, as it shifted behind cover, hiding: it was the sound of a dragging body, hurt, and desperate… the nightmare you'd come to find, we knew.

You turned back to meet my eyes, your hand lifting to place its index finger over your lips in the universal sign of silence, waiting for me to nod, before you started to ease soundlessly into the darkness. Your acute ears somehow knowing where it came from, despite the cavern's endless echo.

How every*thing* sounded like it came from every*where*.

I followed right behind you, trying to slightly tone down my light so whatever we were nearing wouldn't know we *were* coming closer. Letting one of my hands come to rest gently between your shoulder blades so you'd know exactly where I was: trying to hide how it shook, my fingers closing around the soft fabric covering you. My feet feeling heavy, afraid of the sound and what it meant, struggling to keep my lengthened strides long and steady to keep you in reach. Close enough to know, if something bad happened, I'd at least have a chance to possibly protect *you*.

Or, to at least *feel* like I'd be able to.

We paused likely fifteen feet further into the cavern, in a darkness only faintly lit by my light, when the groan came much closer than before: on the other side of a wide formation to our righthand side. A thick column that must have been at least ten feet around, completely solid, reaching all the way up to the ceiling above. It was one of many similar to it in the cavern, as though they alone held up the mountains.

You met my eyes, your hand finding my side to tell me to stay safely back as you eased around. To let your squinted eyes find the hurt, weak, emaciated body hidden on the other side, as soon as you'd rounded the column: a sense of what was almost pity nearly coming over you at the sight, before you could turn it away.

Nearly, but not quite, when you knew what it was.

"What in Hell…" Your voice rumbled through the caverns long after you'd spoken, barely over a whisper yet reverberating around the formations built up around us until it sounded like there were millions of you. It was a form you'd recognized, of course, but it only vaguely resembled the being it had been in the nightmares of before.

Now a barely human, truly skeletal body.

A gruesome sight you actually hid from me when I tried to see through your eyes, even if you knew I would soon see it on my own. Closing the short distance between us carefully, hesitantly: taking your calm tone as a sign that I *could* come to your side without being in the way of any type of fight, that the sight would just be unpleasant. But, I didn't realize quite *how* unpleasant until I had stepped even halfway around the formation, and by then it was much too late to take it back, already deeply regretting my decision—because, I couldn't stop my eyes from flitting over what had once been a strong form, but was now slumped and barely staying upright, appearing as if it had been lost in a state of decay for a very long time.

It likely *had* been for months... ever since we last left it behind.

One of my hands snapped up to cover my lips when a startled gasp escaped, trying to stifle the sound. But, even after looking away the image stayed burned in my mind, the pity you pushed aside coming over me freely—despite knowing what that shadow had done in the past—as my focus forcefully shifted back to the side of your face, my breaths short and fast, wanting only to see you.

To see that you were still doing alright.

I'd seen how the bright crimson dripped down the shadow's face, nearly every inch of it. With what little skin was left in sight so pale it had reached the point of being absolutely transparent, leaving nothing to hide of the white bones beneath. Skin that was tighter than it should be, in a way that drew tears instantly to my eyes: the sight of starvation, even on such a vastly different face, was always far too close to the awful memory of my beautiful sister's past. Whenever I see someone in that state, her face is all I can see. It made its eyes, the dark black spheres without a soul, seem bigger as if they were bulging from their sockets. Made its lips thinner, cracked and colorless, in a way that showcased how it'd lost quite a few of its teeth, with hardly any left: when it opened its mouth it seemed as a bloody, dark cave, not truly a mouth at all. With its thin body, covered in blood and absolutely skeletal, bent over in a way that showcased how its head had started to lose hair, left only in thin patches, as though from an illness.

It was honestly the worst sight I'd ever seen.

And, the only positive thing I could find or feel to the sight, stood in the knowledge of what its frailty meant: in the knowledge that it was weak, because it was *dying*... and, that meant it was losing its hold on this world. That it would lose its hold on you; its hold on us. But, what its desperation would make it soon try to do, because of that, overpowered the positivity.

The negative that you had strongly warned me of.

Its eyes, seeming endlessly deep and dark in the eerie lighting, lifted to find mine as soon as they had left the sight of it. I *felt* their weight on my face, heard the guttural gurgling growl it started to make at the sight of me, when I stepped around the pillar. Saw how you shifted to place yourself between me and them the moment I was with you, letting them see only what wasn't hidden behind you.

Making my hand rise to once again find your back, now openly shaking.

The nightmare's voice was raspy, in a way that soundly strangely *far* too wet, more a hiss than words at all. It spoke between breaths, every word sounding just as in pain as it appeared to be, "You won't even... *look*? To see, *what* you have... done? We were almost... free to take back what's... ours. *Our* land, *our* sea. But, *you*... were too *selfish*... to get rid of even a *little*... of that *fucking* light... Selfish... witch."

"Love," My voice was barely audible, my hand closing tightly around your shirt. Trying to show you the words I knew it wouldn't let me speak. You shifted your gaze to mine, but kept *it* in sight: as my mind showed you. "We—"

"Quiet... *witch*. No one wants... to *hear* you. No one *ever* wants... to hear *your* sad little... *useless* words." The nightmare's voice was louder than before, enough to echo through the cavern far longer than it should have. Rougher and deeper in a way that made my eyes close: trying to ignore the awful cold starting to settle over me. "It's *your* fault... *he's* taken our *world*. The... *animal* who doesn't even... *belong* here. No... He *doesn't*... belong *anywhere*. We... *tried*. We tried... and *will* try... and *will*..."

You reached back to find the side of my hip, your hand closing around my skirt to draw me closer. I came to you the moment you asked, my free hand finding the side of your waist as I pressed tight to your back. Being wherever you needed me to be, trying to be ready to do whatever you would need me to do.

Whenever the time came.

"We *will*... take it *back*. And, *you*..." A laugh rattled in its throat, its eyes lifting to find yours. And, you met them without flinching. Showing a complete lack of what it wanted from you, more than anything: weakness, and fear. "*You* won't... *be* here. No... no, you should *never*... have *been* here. An unwanted pest... who we *will*... rid *our* land of... to... *reclaim* what is... *ours*."

It turned to cough toward the ground, violently, loudly. And, it coughed for far too long... until the sound became a manic laugh. Not caring about, rather only laughing at, the heavier flow of bright crimson that came dripping rapidly down its chin. I had glanced back down as it did, when the cough wouldn't end, even if I knew I shouldn't. When a part of me knew it had been waiting for me to: beginning to laugh only when my eyes dropped to see. Letting me, unfortunately, see as it spit out a few more teeth, losing half of the few it'd carried before. Letting us watch, as it roughly pushed back up to lean against the column—making sure we both saw as its hideous face suddenly transformed into an even *more* monstrously deteriorated form, even when such a thing should have been impossible; as its thin skin started to far too-quickly sag as though it had forgotten how to be a part of the bones at all, starting to truly tear itself apart.

And, so fast: far too fast.

"The end is coming, sad little boy... for *all* of us. Her... *light*," It spat the word out with a tooth, as if it were the worst word in existence: but, considering it was likely the cause to its state, it probably really was the worst thing to the nightmare. "It won't save *you*... won't save *anyone*. No... It will... *it* will destroy us... and, *you*, sad little boy... will be nothing... not until *you*... *extinguish*... that *fucking light*... for good." More coughing, "We will *show*... you. *Let* us... show you..." It laughed, that far too bloody laugh, "*You're* just a *key*... to an *end*. You... are just... a *disappointment*."

My hand tightened around your side, trying to bring your eyes back to mine. But, you refused to look away... telling me that *thing* was already messing with your head, as that type of cruel shadow exists only to do—trying to tear down and destroy, in the worst possible way, all the *good* spirits.

Those who hurt the most.

"Love," I spoke softly, barely a whisper, ignoring everything except you: watching your brows furrow, in a way that told me you still *heard* me, at least, but were having to fight to keep some control of your beautiful mind. "It isn't—"

It interrupted with a louder laugh, coughing harshly after. Making my hands tighten on you even more, jumping closer, my eyes squeezing shut. "*They* say light's... *good*. But, it *destroys*. We *knew* when... *you* first came *here*... what *he* would... let *you* do. The... *poison* you'd... spread. We tried to... *stop* it, before it... began. To *lock* you... in. But... *you* trapped the *animal* before we... could. *Used* him. A *wall* we couldn't... *break*. Used the... *light* so we couldn't... find *you*. Now... *you* bring *us* light... to *destroy* our kind. Claiming to be *good*... but *trying* to... to..."

"To stop things like you from hurting him." My eyes rose to meet its, blazing with a fury they rarely hold. The indescribable fury that comes when we see one another in pain: when I saw you falling into a haze that had to be broken. I unflinchingly met its grotesque face, stepping in front of you to block most of you from its sight, just as you had for me. "You think I can't see the truth, don't you?"

"*Truth*? When you're... a *delusion*?" It laughed that awful laugh, making me hate that *thing* more than I hated anything. "*Tell* the *truth*, then... tell *him* what he *did*... when he—"

"Don't say another word, you... you lying sack of shit." I stared into its eyes, ignoring the hideous face, the skin hanging from its skull: I only saw the truth of what it was, as only we could. "*All* you are is a lie—a vile *thing* that won't exist after we—"

It laughed, again, "Then, you... *will* always be... alone, *witch*. And, he—"

"*He*. Is. Everything." I *felt* my light, filling the space with an intensity it never had before: and, felt the weight of your barely conscious gaze heavily on me, listening to me, watching me. "*He* is good, and *kind*. Honest, and brave. And, he'll *always* be mine... so, no, I'll *never* be alone."

The nightmare laughed, that rattling, cold sound: as the true nightmare we'd known had been hiding inside, the tall haze of suffocating smoke, began to free itself of its disguise. Its eyes becoming a flaming bright red, as the smoke broke free of its body. "We'll... see, won't... *we*?"

That was when it moved, and time slowed.

I saw your arm reach from behind me, wrapping around my torso to keep *me* from taking what it was about to do, before I could stop you. Sacrificing yourself, to protect me, as you always do. Holding your hand right over my heart, to shield where you had known the shadow would target. Letting the nightmare, instead, take ahold of you. I wasn't fast enough to push your arm back, to stop you *or* it, before it suddenly leaned forward, too, closing the distance: I couldn't stop one of its hands from catching ahold of your wrist, over your watch—shielding my heart with the part of *you* that you knew it would most want to hurt, that it wouldn't hesitate to accept instead of me—holding you so tightly your arm instantly reddened around it.

I only had time for my hand to land right over its, but was *helpless* to stop it, to take you away. Before it all came in a flash, my mind hardly even registering it had: as that hand found your skin, and mine fell over its, I tried to make my light burst out of me, trying to wrap around you and push it away, but nothing came; I felt the cold ice of its cruel skin trying to take the warmth of yours… and then I was thrown away from you, by a scream like none other I had ever heard before, tearing out of that shadow with a force like none I'd ever felt before. Its touch on *your* skin making a surge of pain rip straight through *my* head, through all of my body, making my light suddenly flicker out—its darkness stopping my light from doing what it wanted to—just before I was hit by a hard burst of cold wind that threw me *far* across the caverns. Far away from *you*. My numb flight only stopping when my back slammed into something, sending my body falling limply to the cold ground.

Sending the world into darkness.

I could only lay there, cold and unfeeling. Literally frozen. As that awful *thing* took control of your mind. Seeing through your eyes, when mine were blinded by darkness, as though it were *truly* happening to me. Watching, how your eyes were locked on your arm as you instantly pulled it free. Watching, how that redness grew across your skin, traveling up your arm as the too-hot feeling of a furious fire spread from your wrist all the way to your shoulder, turning *bright* red before our eyes. But, more than anything, I *felt* as your face, your body, your *entire* being was overtaken by that horrible pain: the heartbreaking agony of one who feels *lost*.

I watched—unable to do *anything*—as the cruel nightmare forced you to see things you should never have to see: images I'd witnessed when that heartbreaking pain had taken over you before, and never wanted to see again. Making you see a flood of dark crimson flowing from where it had touched you, that sent a raging pain through all of you... a pain that you'd felt to your very soul when it had happened in the past.

A pain that shattered my heart both then, and now.

"No..." Your voice echoed through my entire world: the desperate sob that I had no power to remedy. As your hand snapped over the horrible downpour of crimson, your eyes squeezing shut, trying to be as blind as mine were.

Reaching out to me, with all that you had, for help.

That was when I suddenly saw that situation with different eyes, neither truly my own or yours: but the eyes of *our* spirit. Eyes that could see more than any other may. Watching as that thing stood and reached out to you, not with a hand but with smoke, enveloping all of you in true darkness, trying to *take* you from me. As it became what it truly was, forgetting the fading guise it had held all your life. Growing taller, to the very height of the caverns, as all that was left of its skin sloughed away from its bones and then let those bones turn to dust. To free that cold, *empty* smoke.

Becoming the faceless form of a black-hearted nightmare.

Then... I felt you *fall*, and heard you call out my name. With a desperation, fear and agony that could have made me move the entire world to reach you, to take that pain away from you before it could take you away from the world—I felt the shift in ways that can't possibly be explained, felt *myself* change from who I had been, into who I always needed to be. Who you had always known I was, and could be. Easily thawing through the cold that had kept me frozen, breaking through anything that tried to stop me, with the fear that I could possibly *lose* you.

My Everything.

Letting a strong surge of energy, *our* energy, throw me to where I needed to be, as that light *burst* out of me. A light that cut easily through the thick darkness, the smoke around me—a light that lit up the entire world, with *our* light: cleansing the land of all the darkness that had ever touched it… shining light in every corner.

As I let all of myself become our *spirit*.

I was on my feet before the thought entered my mind—before I remembered I had a body separate from yours—as I felt my light coming back to the surface, becoming all that I am. As I, for the first time, found the power to *create* something in a dream, and altered our world: forever. Rising from the cold, hard ground and stepping into a part of our world that was far beyond the caverns. Where the source of that energy had truly escaped from, where the darkness and nightmares *all* escaped from. Taking myself to where I needed to be, without my mind even having a conscious thought to get there: to where I knew *it* had taken you. Because, for the very first time in my life, I wasn't afraid to face them… not even in a hallway.

Because, that hallway, was now filled by our light.

If one didn't *know* it was the same world that had tormented us as children, it would seem impossible to believe it was. Though, this was the first time that I was able to truly see it at all, so that may not have been true to everyone: perhaps, it was more like someone had come along and flipped a light-switch, or drawn back the drapes to let the sun clear the dust, fog and darkness from the forgotten halls of an abandoned building that had long existed without the feeling of life, of love, beating in its walls. Revealing the same image it had been before, but now with the honest and cherished truth of what it was meant to be.

With its heart shining for *all* to see.

But, where once those hallways had been winding, dark, and cold, a seemingly endless maze of sorrow that housed all the spirits who had forgotten how to hope, how to find their way home, trapped by a darkness that wouldn't set them free… now, those doors I could never pry open lined only one wall, with long windows lining the entire length of the other, revealing a view of the beautiful city—a part of our world which I don't mention in this dream, except for here, but a piece of our world that plays a great part in most our dreams—bustling with life below, letting the warm sun *bring* its life to all who had once been trapped behind the shadows.

Filling the hallways with a light that revealed how, in its honest and free form as it now was, it would have easily fit into a hotel: with walls lined by light cream-colored wallpaper, embellished with details of shining golden flowers; with thick, soft red carpet covering the floors that sank welcomingly beneath my feet.

With doors that no longer shook as the trapped tried to find their way desperately free, that no longer had clawing, cruel hands reaching out to stop me. Preventing me from doing what we could to help the lost. Now, instead of gray and crumbling, those doors were a smooth, glossy white, with most standing freely open to reveal all of the bright, safe rooms that had once been concealed behind them. The rooms that we now knew how to *keep* safe, in the light: rooms that would protect all those who needed to find their way, until they regained their footing and found their path.

Rooms that let me see all the beautifully smiling, happy spirits now residing inside. How their eyes lifted to meet mine as I passed, looking at me all the same when I kept my eyes forward after the first couple doors. Looking at me with a hope in their eyes, a glittering happiness and peace, that made me feel as though I were floating.

Making me feel as *light* as I glowed.

Walking down the hallway steadily, unafraid. With one hand at my side, its palm open to face the way ahead of me as though holding someone's hand, openly giving my light to the world just as the sun gave that light to me: sharing the warmth and the hope of that light with anyone I passed. Making all those who had happened to be out of their rooms in my crossing stop what they were doing as I passed by them, to stare at me, too, just as those in the rooms were. With bright smiles lighting up their faces as I *did* pass them by: shifting out of my way as I came towards them, just enough to not interfere with my path, and looking at me with that hope... a gratitude that I can't explain in words, which made me feel just as warm *as* the sun.

Walking with an undeniable confidence that could have told anything within a great radius of that hallway that nothing would be able to stop me from doing what I'd have to do. Calmly and surely, despite the bow that had appeared in my left hand as soon as I stepped into the hallway, with an arrow resting between my fingers, waiting.

Because, I knew what that arrow would *do*.

It was at the end of the hallway that I came upon what I knew I would find: the closed double doors leading into what was surely a ballroom sized room beyond. A room that honestly cannot be described in its grandness, but I will try for visualization sake: the doors themselves stood at the height of what had to be three of me, with the ceilings within rising *far* higher, into a vaulted dome made of glass overhead; with floors of shining marble, and walls painted with art truly beyond description. Of hills, rivers, mountains, cities... people smiling, laughing, and loving.

Art made by *you*, and your beautiful mind.

My strides didn't slow, didn't even shorten, pushing both doors open without even touching them as the wind and light radiating around my body did so for me. My steps leading me right to the middle of that room, as my hand drew that bow in front of me, the other easily nocking the arrow on its string.

All my eyes saw were you, how you were tightly curled in a ball at the center of that room, sparking a protective wave through me that would have made it possible for me to do anything. Anything to get to *you*. Sparking a hatred for that cruel, dark shadow—the only one left in our world—hovering over you, speaking words that should never be heard, words to make even the strongest give up... sparking a wave that gave us the power to get rid of it, completely.

And, I didn't wait... for anything.

"Quiet, asshole. No one wants to hear you." I spoke between my teeth, drawing the arrow back, my aim perfectly centered on that thing's chest. My words making its red eyes snap away from you, my

Love, taking its attention away from you: enough away from you that I had a perfect shot without fear of hitting *you*.

But, I knew it wouldn't.

My eyes narrowed, my fingers starting to relax. Releasing a steady exhale, even as I continued to close the distance between us, as I released that arrow: letting it slam through its chest, through its heart had it had one, through *all* of it. Stronger than an arrow should logically be. But, that very arrow wasn't a normal arrow at all: it was an arrow made by a woman who finally realized that our world *was* hers to control, too, even when she had doubted her ability to do so all her life… no matter how often you assured her she could—the ability to choose who walked its lands and who didn't. An arrow carrying a vow that nothing cruel would ever walk our sacred lands again.

Throwing it far away from *you*, far away from our world, forever.

But, as what that vile thing had once been fell away into nothing, I didn't spare it a glance: before it was gone I'd fallen beside you, over you. My only focus was *you*, beside me but still trapped within nightmares—with your face twisted in utter agony, and your lips parted to create a moan, your entire body rocking with strained breaths. Holding your legs close to appear smaller; with one arm beneath your head, its hand keeping a death-grip on your hair, and the other held tightly over your waist as if you'd just been punched, clutching at your shirt, in front of your belly.

My hands gently found either side of your face, tilting you towards mine.

"Don't you *dare* leave me… you're not allowed to." I let that light twist around all of you, holding your own energy to me, giving you all

I had. "I'm not *letting* you, my Love."

I leant down to meet your lips, sending every drop of my love into you. Our light's heat spreading out from my hand as my aura wrapped *through* all of you, mending all that'd been broken with a rapidity and surety I'd never held before, healing you inside and out as no one else can. Protecting you as only I can.

As my mind drifted into dark memories that weren't my own.

It started with brief flashes from hundreds of moments, a barrage of horrible images I hadn't seen in years. Horrors my mind didn't want to believe possible: flashes of you as a sweet, scared, hurt, lost, *innocent* child being abused by one who was supposed to protect you; a horrible movie merging all the way through into newer scenes with new antagonists as you grew older, but carried no less hurt—images that made me feel just as helpless as that little boy was, carrying me in the darkness until I was finally able to step out of the background, and bring our light into the nightmare.

Stepping into a room without any identifying details: a dark, empty room with no doors or furniture, just dark gray walls and floors. A room so cold that I could see my every breath, with a layer of fog sweeping across the floors and down from the walls, as though trapped in a freezer. A room, where a scared little boy sat all alone in a dark corner, with his knees hugged into his chest and his face buried in his arms, crying.

I crossed the room as soon as I entered it, making my way to kneel on both knees in front of you. So close, that my skirt puddled across your bare feet: a contact that made your fast, sobbing breaths first hitch, and then slowly start to calm. As my hand softly found where one of your hands tightly clutched your elbow, letting my thumb tenderly sweep over your skin. Easing those sobs, until you were able to take your head from the cover of your arms, to meet my eyes.

Looking at me as you always do: as *your* everything.

A small smile crossed my lips as you did, to show you everything was alright. That *you* were alright. Meeting your beautiful eyes for just a moment—seeing a flash of the hope, relief… of undeniable love, brimming to the surface of those eyes—before you threw yourself at me. Throwing me back to sit on my legs as your arms wrapped tight around my waist, holding your ear securely to my heart: hugging me so fiercely, that I couldn't stop the tears tumbling freely down my cheeks as my arms wrapped around you, too, holding you safely to me.

Tears that flowed faster when you spoke. In the small, young voice that I had grown up knowing better than my own. Feeling the words run through all of me, even when they were spoken so softly. Words that were muffled by how you kept your face in my chest, "Was so dark… before *you*."

"I know, baby… but, it won't ever be dark again. I promise you." One of my hands gently found the back of your head, holding you to my heart. As the other hand left your back to reach into a pocket of my skirts, to withdraw something that definitely hadn't been there before: a candlestick, holding a single white candle. Slowly drawing you away from my chest as that arm wrapped around your torso, to gently take one of your arms from my waist. Letting me place the candle in your small hand, keeping my own securely around yours, my eyes staying on *yours* as you studied the candle. "Any time you're afraid, you'll see its flame. You'll see my love… and know you aren't alone. Alright?"

You nodded. Those eyes slightly widening as I lit that candle without touching it, simply with my mind, filling the room with its soft glow. A glow that slowly began to bring detail to that cold room, turning it into a *safe*, warm bedroom. As you brought the candle closer, so close it nearly touched your nose, "What if it goes out?"

"It won't, my darling… our candle burns with a love that will *never* fade." My hand gently found the side of your face, to bring those beautiful eyes back to mine. Letting my eyes tell you everything. "With a light, that will *always* show you the way home."

That magnificent smile crossed your face, lighting those eyes, "Always?"

"And, forever, sweet baby." I leant down to softly kiss your forehead, letting my eyes fall closed. Keeping my lips against you as I spoke, "*Come home.*"

You did, as soon as I asked it, throwing us safely back into the world of our dream's reality—back to *you*, my Everything.

I drew away, just far enough to let the tip of my nose touch yours. My hands staying on either side of your perfect face, letting my thumbs softly feather over your cheeks, asking you to wake without startling you out of the nightmare, "Come back to me, my Love."

Watching, as those beautiful eyes slowly opened to meet mine.

Letting us simply stare at one another, with our soft breaths flowing in a united rhythm, until your lips parted to say words you weren't able to truly create. Until your breaths quickened, as your beautiful eyes started to glass over: your emotions worn down after what you had just experienced in those nightmares.

Worn down after *everything* that had happened that night.

"No... my Love. No." I let myself fall into you, as soon as your eyes turned glassy, keeping our faces together: nestling all of me tighter to you until our bodies, laying on our sides on that cool marble, fit perfectly into one another's. Keeping my hands just where they were, my thumbs catching your tears, as my own started to flow down my cheeks, too. "Everything's alright now, baby. *You're* alright."

Your heavy hand slowly came to rest on my back, holding me as if you were afraid to touch me, as if the simplest touch would hurt me: those eyes studying me as though we may both vanish at any second, and you didn't want to forget a single detail.

Studying me, just as I studied you.

I softly kissed to the side of your lips. Nuzzling your face with my nose as a deeper, shaky breath ran through you. "You're okay... we're *both* okay."

Your other hand slowly, gently, lifted to find the side of my face, letting your thumb sweep the trail of tears delicately away from my skin. But, you said nothing except the worried words in your eyes: except, the deep well of guilt I felt rising inside you.

"Talk to me, Love." I nuzzled you again, "Please... talk to me?"

Your beautiful voice was hoarse, broken, "I hurt you."

"No. No, Love, you *didn't*." I shook my head quickly as you nodded, as that guilt crossed your beautiful face. "I'm worried about you. Felt helpless and scared, and I… I didn't know what to do. But, you didn't…" My voice broke when your eyes closed, letting a new heartbreaking stream of tears leak from their corners. Making my words more a sob than words at all, "No. Please, Love, don't cry. Oh, baby, *no*…"

Your hand slid down my back to find the fabric at my hips, closing tightly around my skirt as a broken sound went through you in place of the words you tried to form: a sound that shattered my whole world.

"Love…" I kissed away those tears, kissing every last inch of your beautiful face; my hands truly cradling your face. Showering you in all my love, since I didn't know what else to do. But, you stopped me when I was shy of finding your lips, your hand leaving my face to find the back of my throat. To gently pull me into the crook of your own: burying your face in my hair, folding your body entirely around mine.

Clinging to me as you, my strong Love, fell apart.

My arm looped around your neck to hold you tighter to me, protectively, feeling your warm tears flowing freely on my throat. Making my body curl even closer to you in an attempt to show you that you had me, whatever you may need. Making your hold tighten around me, too, your tears flowing faster: and, all I could do was squeeze my eyes shut, letting tears stream freely down my own cheeks as my arms wrapped even more around you, holding you as safely as I could.

Protecting you, as you released all you had buried inside.

Staying just that way until you buried your face even tighter into my neck. Until a horrible, hurt sound left you that made my eyes blink open, my hold slightly loosening as what you needed dawned on me: as what I could *do* to help heal your pain suddenly became the clearest thought in the world. What I could do to show you weren't alone, and never *would* be—that you never had to deal with your pain or troubles, no matter what they were, alone again.

To show you, that you're safe.

My hand slowly left your throat to slide tenderly over your shoulder. Gliding down your chest and across your stomach as I shifted to rest on my knees beside you, urging you to draw your face away from me. You did, hesitantly. Your brows furrowing, until you realized what I had that moment before, knowing what I was going to do with just one glance at my eyes: making your entire body still, those tears simply ceasing, your breaths hitching. All the above making a small smile cross my lips, knowing I really *had* found the way to cure every pain you may ever possess... by showing you just how much you're loved, for being *you*.

My other hand found yours—already lifted to help me, just as you knew I'd need you—steadying my balance as I shifted to straddle you. Letting my body lower on top of yours, my chest coming lower to yours, as my other hand found your belt and freed all between me and you. As my lips slowly trailed their way tenderly up your throat, along your jawline, to kiss every inch of your beautiful face, erasing those tears.

Your voice was even more hoarse than before, "Y'don't have to, if you…"

"Shh, my Love." I met your eyes, already affected by me as I hoped they would be. Kissing your lips sweetly, briefly, before pulling just far enough away to meet your eyes again. Letting my forehead rest against yours, "Let me *help* you, my Love."

Your hands glided up my thighs to find my either hip as I positioned myself closer over you. As I kissed every inch of you other than your beautiful lips. A tender assault that made your hoarse voice breathy, your hands tightening around my hips, "M'sorry y'had to… Don't know why I… reacted that way. I—"

"It's alright, my Love." My teeth caught ahold of your bottom lip to effectively stop your apology, gently tugging before I slowly released it to kiss you. My eyes staying on yours, "Nothing will ever come between us again."

You kissed me, slowly and deeply as you always do, and just a bit roughly: completely filled with your magnificent love. Shifting your hips beneath me as your deft tongue found mine, needing me just as much as you always do, trying to urge me to close the distance between us with more than just my hand, but I wasn't yet giving what you wanted.

Not until you weren't blaming yourself, for things that weren't your fault.

You drew slightly away, keeping my lips against yours: those eyes vulnerable as no one else ever sees them. Your words a vow, "Won't hurt y'again, m'Life."

"You never *have*, my Love." Your strong hands tightened around my hips, openly impatient. But, I only kissed the tip of your nose, "They're just lucky that I'll probably never meet them. Those who hurt *you*... would learn how protective I am."

You gently caught my bottom lip between your teeth, doing as I had to you not long ago. Before, I let myself slowly sit up, to *truly* straddle you. Taking both your hands in mine, as you breathlessly spoke, "Don't want t'talk 'bout m'fucking—fuck, m'Life."

That ridiculous smile crossed my face: one of pride, of triumph.

"I *love* you, my Love. So *incredibly* much." I recaptured your lips the moment you sat up, too, to do just that. Kissing you with all I am, as you started to move with me. My tongue easily parting your lips to find yours, kissing you as deeply as I could. As I took all of you just the same: as I showed you the way back up to the stars and yet further, giving you absolutely everything.

Everything and more.

"I *love* you... more than anything." I spoke at that volume only you can hear, my lips kissing your collar-bone. "Don't *ever* leave me, okay?"

We stayed just as we were before, only still: I didn't have any desire to leave where I was, safely in your lap with my legs crossed behind you, wrapped in your arms; with you securely around me, a part of me, safe in my arms. Wrapped in the calm security of knowing our Everything is safe, with us—we didn't even realize, until later, that at some point we had returned to the caverns... now just as peaceful as they're meant to be.

"You know I'd never…" Your hand tenderly found the side of my face, drawing me out from beneath your chin to meet my eyes—your own still welling with tears, just as mine were—unable to finish your words; only able to release a heavy breath in their place.

But, your eyes told me everything: they always do.

"I *do* know, Love." I flattened one of my hands on your chest, right over your perfect heart. Letting my lips find yours, to say more than words ever can, as your hands found either side of my face… saying those unspoken words in the only way you were able to.

The only way we ever really want to.

Kissing me deeply, passionately and desperately, as one only can when they've just been scared, and amazed in the matter of seconds. Making a soft moan, the most content, happiest, most grateful sound I had ever made, leave me when you did, my body truly melting into yours as your deft tongue easily parted my lips to take all of me in that kiss. To give me everything you had.

And, you only pulled away when you absolutely had to, "Y'don't know how much I love *you, my* Love."

"More than the whole rest of the world can love anything?"

"Yeah." That perfect smile quirked over your lips, "Something like that."

"Then, I may have an idea." I kept my nose alongside yours, my lips against yours in that way you had taught me. Making every word a kiss. "I definitely love *you* more than the rest of the world can possibly love anything."

"Truly… don't know what I'd do without you, my Life." Your

teary eyes softened even more on mine, your hand leaving my face to find the small of my back: skin that was bare to you. "Don't know how fucking terrified I was."

"I know, Love." My eyes fell briefly down to your nose. Speaking in a shaky breath, barely audibly, "I was, too."

Your eyes filled with a guilt unlike any I'd ever seen before, "Did they—"

"No. Love, no." I kissed you, long and slow, telling you just how alright I was, so long as I have you. Making sure my eyes didn't leave yours, to show you the depth of my words: how you hadn't *only* saved me from taking the brunt of those nightmares. "You saved me. *All* of me, my Love. You know that... pretty sure you see it, too?"

"Y'mean the bright sun 'round you? Yeah, I *might've* noticed that." You gently drew me away, to let you study every inch of my face. Again, as though it would be the last time that you could. Letting your eyes shine with incomparable sincerity, "Y'saved me, too. Always do... You know that, yeah? That y'really are everything, to me."

"And, *you* really are everything to me." I came back to kiss you, "I *love* you."

"More than anything."

"Everything." I kissed you, once again long and slow, giving you all I had. My eyes flicking over every inch of your beautiful, perfect face just as yours had to mine that moment before. "Are you alright? Honestly."

A smile quirked over your lips, "M'perfect, m'light."

"Absolutely perfect..." I kissed your nose, "But, I meant, can you walk?"

"Yeah?" You drew me back to you, kissing me between your every single word. "Among many other things. Whatever y'need m'to. Why?"

"Well, Katie's still probably waiting."

You didn't stop kissing me, "Yeah, probably."

"So, we should probably get going. Soon as possible."

"Sure... soon as possible."

"Love." A light laugh left me, just as you had hoped it would, as I drew slightly away. "Trust me, you can kiss me and I can kiss you all we want. But, *after* Katie. And, well, everything else. You know we —"

"Yeah. Everything." You kissed me several more times before I drew reluctantly away from you. Slowly making my way out of your lap, and all the way up to my feet, catching one of your hands in mine to help you to *your* feet after I rose to my own, before we could be just as distracted once more.

As we deeply wanted to be.

You came with me easily, proving how fine you were, slinging an arm heavily over my shoulders once we were to draw me securely to your side. Quirking your brow, when I looked up at you, "Jus' t'be clear, was that a'promise?"

"Mhm." I smiled, rising slightly onto my toes to kiss your chin, "I *love* you, my crazy, beautiful man. And, I *promise*, I'm going to show you so, in every way possible."

"Yeah?"

My smile grew to that likely goofy state, "Yeah."

"Alright, then." You started to lead me to wherever the exit of those caverns was: I didn't question the direction, simply trusting you. Thankfully, since you didn't exactly let me see anything except you, leaning down to continue kissing me. And, somehow, doing so easily despite how we walked. Speaking breathlessly between kissing, unwilling to pull away even for a second: we really do need one another like air. "We'll find your sister."

"Hm, but I thought you weren't in a hurry?"

"M'not. But, I *do*," You turned to walk backwards, drawing me tight to you—which would have been difficult, if we didn't always walk in the same stride—showing me just how much, how and why you meant it. "Want you *home*, Danie."

I drew you back down, to kiss you, "Then take me home, my Love."

We kissed long and deeply as we left the caverns, and the nightmares that once hid inside, behind. To face the world and whatever may be waiting outside with newfound confidence, with a surety that no matter what we really *would* be fine.

Because, we would be united—always.

Fresh air had never felt as freeing as it did when we stepped out of the caves. The magnificent view beyond seeming as though we stepped right into summer-land, into heaven, making the trance we travelled in seem even more magical than it had before.

We stood at the edge of a narrow ridge of the mountain, looking out over a beautiful valley painted by the soft pinks and purples of the sky: a divine show of light casting gracefully down from the sun as it began to slowly set, lowering over the gentle hills rolling into the distance and down to the sea.

Over a world of unbelievable greens and blues.

Where the magnificent, treeless mountains became the gentle hills of a valley, stray woods started to rise from the Earth. And, through and around those trees, the soft blue of a river wound steadily through the green: the same river that we had followed from the quarry, winding gracefully from the mountains out to the bright blue bay, that lead out to the sea, and to the village at the bay's far off edge.

Only a single narrow road wound between the mountains, through the valley and out to the open hills beyond. Flowing with the natural way of the land, on its way to find the town, only broken by a bridge crossing a smaller stream of water leading to the bay. With just a few stray homes dotting the hills in our far off sight, small cottages surrounded by smooth green grass with only a few patches of trees left to dot the land, most with out-buildings around the main home, their barns and sheds: with tiny living dots moving over the fields and valleys.

A quiet world, of farms and animals.

You silently studied me as I took in that view. Never once looking away from me to see what was beyond us, as my eyes flitted over every last detail in pure wonder, my lips parted in awe. Standing at my side, with my hand tight around yours, as a gentle, wonderful warmth filled us: the sense of all things simply being *right*... a feeling that I only feel at your side. Because, we knew, even in a dream where some would say it wasn't the "true" sight, that magnificent view was part of your home—*our* home.

And, well, that means it's perfect… to me.

My gaze left the sight in search of yours, not hiding how my eyes instantly filled with new wonder, with an even greater happiness. Shining with the bright, undeniable love that always enters our eyes whenever we see one another: a love that perfectly reflected yours.

Because, *you* will always be my home.

My voice was soft as air, as if speaking louder could dispel the enchantment of that view, of where we were. "It always seems too perfect to be real. But, *is*."

Your smile, resting contentedly across your lips for as long as I'd been looking at the valley, twitched higher to crinkle the skin around your glittering eyes as you lifted a hand to brush stray strands of my hair from my face. Tucking it tenderly behind my ear, and letting your touch linger when I leant into you. My happy eyes closing, as you spoke. "It's home, m'heart."

"Mm, *you* are." I shifted even closer to you, squeezing our entwined hands. As my other hand rose to rest right over your heart, its palm over your breast to feel its steady beat, your calm. Your happiness. "From the first breath I took, I've known that."

"Likewise." Your knuckles feathered softly across the side of my face. Far more tenderly than one should have the power to be, yet you always manage. Letting that hand find the side of my throat, your thumb gently tilting my face up to yours: to let you see just how brightly my eyes shone for you, sparkling like snow under the sun.

Letting me see just how extravagantly yours shone for me.

Making a smile find its way across my lips… my eyes rising to the sky when I felt something cold softly land on my nose. As the sky suddenly began to release delicate flecks of snow, the moment that thought—that sweet comparison—crossed your mind, simply because *we* had wanted it to. "This world really *is* us, isn't it? Everything… it's us."

"Yeah." Your fingertips swept another stray curl out from my face—it *was* decently windy, where we were—tucking it gently back behind my ear. A small, sweet smile crossing your lips when my eyes came back to meet yours, "You're everything."

"*We* are, my Love." I let my fingers slide under the neckline of your shirt, to find your warm skin, your perfect heart. To feel the pulse of your beautiful life. *My* life. "We're both the bright sun, and the graceful moon. The safe Earth, and the gentle sky. The warm soil and the cool sea… we are both the angel above the sky, and the spirit walking the Earth down below. Guiding, and protecting one another, to make sure we find our way, in every life we have… *You* are my life, my Love. My everything."

"Yeah… likewise." You closed the distance between your lips and mine. Letting your lips continue to brush softly over my own, as the tip of your index finger rose to gently feather over one of my eyes, over my lashes, "Knew y'were everything in m'life when I first saw you. Was *those* eyes… made me yours before y'were even born."

I turned to kiss that hand, "I was yours long before."

"We *always* were each other's, my light." Your hand glided slowly down to find the exposed upper-part of my shoulder, taking up all the space I had to offer, and more: your perfect skin gliding gently over mine in a way that sent a shiver over me, done just so. I didn't hide the content sound that left me as you did, as you gently turned my body to fully face yours. "Will always remember the first night I looked at the stars... as if it was all I lived t'see. As if it were a'logical thing t'do."

"It was, wasn't it?"

"Sure was." You let the tip of your nose touch mine, still leaving just your eyes in sight. "Was the first I saw you, when awake... and would've missed you, if I listened to him calling me insane. When he found m'staring at the sky."

"You'd never miss me, Love."

"No, m'dear. Not for the world." Your smile grew with sweet happiness, reaching high enough to crinkle those eyes. The sight I would do absolutely anything for. Anything you asked. "If time went by b'tween seeing you, I'd sneak out t'find a place t'see my 'angel' again. That *really* made him think I was insane... but, no, it didn't stop me."

I rested my forehead against yours, "Because, you aren't."

"No." Your fingertips tenderly caressed my skin: your thumb beneath my collar-bone, your fingers over my shoulder-blade. Drawing another happy sound from me. "But, I never did care who thought so. Not even those who say they've proof I am."

"Proof that you're the most sane person alive." My smile grew, as yours did just the same. Tilting my chin up to touch yours, our lips once again barely apart, "And, the most romantic..." I let my lips brush yours, "And, the bravest... *Nothing* can stop you from finding a way to me, even if all the world tries stopping you."

"No." You spoke against me in that magical endless kiss you

perfected, "When you call for me… I don't care what I have t'do t'find you."

"You *always* do." I kissed you, just once and slowly, "I remember you in the rain when you came to me. Far more than once."

"Tends t'rain a'wee bit here, sure."

"*Storming*, I mean. And, the snow."

"Sure." You kissed me, just the same as I'd kissed you, "You're the only thing that's ever mattered t'me… weather be damned."

"Mm…" I drew slightly away, enough to rise onto my toes and kiss the tip of your perfect nose. Drawing a nearly goofy grin across your beautiful face, one that brought mine back into existence, too, as I fell back to my normal height, "Maybe I *do* make you crazy, my Love."

"Oh, undoubtedly." You kissed the tip of *my* nose back, drawing a laugh from me, as your eyes tightened on mine. Speaking in a beautifully over-exaggerated way with your accent, that made a certain part of me respond to every last word. "Y'madden me with your love, m'light."

"Of course I do… *You*," My hand rose to find the side of your face, drawing you down to me. I kissed you, long and sweetly. Making ridiculous grins cross our faces as I drew away, "You, my adorable, crazy, wonderful you, *you* do carry my heart. Don't you?"

"I do. And, *you* carry *mine*. Here." Your hand left my shoulder to find my heart. Taking the opportunity to cup one of my breasts fully in your palm, your fingers caressing the soft skin that escaped my dress. Escaping more than it typically did, as that hand skillfully pushed it slightly higher to do just that. Kissing me as I had you a moment before, your lips staying against my own in that way, each word a kiss. "As only *you* will ever have m'heart, my Life."

"Just as only you, my Love, will ever have mine." I kissed you, "*And*, my spirit." My hand glided from your face, down your chest and stomach, to almost roughly catch ahold on your belt. Tugging you as close to me as it was possible to, making that magnificent smile cross your face. "*And*, my body... you definitely carry that, too."

My lips retook possession of yours, my tongue easily parting your lips to find your own. Never looking away from the beautiful sea of your eyes, not even for a moment. So, when I spoke again my voice was far passed breathless, "I interrupted you, didn't—"

You kissed me, quickly and sweetly, interrupting *me*. The expression over your face when you drew away telling me you'd honestly forgotten about every last thing except what we had been doing a second before.

You shrugged a shoulder, "Said it b'fore, anyway."

"Kinda wanted to hear again... can tell me, as we walk? Should probably get going, before the sun sets." My eyes flicked out to the mountains, the valleys and sea. Trying to take that moment to slip away from you, to avoid getting distracted more than we already had.

But, you stopped me, just as I wanted you to.

"Yeah. *Probably*." You'd easily caught me: I was only able to take my hand from yours and turn halfway to the path leading down the mountain, before your then freed hand found the side of my face to turn me right back. Stopping me in a way I'd never protest: kissing me slow and deep, your tongue finding mine in that way which was nearly rough but wonderfully so, taking all thought of slipping away from my mind. A kiss that made me melt right back into you, as your other arm wrapped around my waist, its hand flat over the small of my back to hold me to you, keeping me there.

Only pulling away from that magnificence to let your eyes meet mine. Your voice husky, lower in a way that definitely didn't help me leave there, "S'you said, we *are* this world, m'Danie. *Time*'s ours, too. There's no reason to hurry, not anymore. Is there?"

"Mm..." My voice was beyond breathless, soft as air. In a way that I know definitely didn't help *you*. "But, the *other* world—"

"By the end of tonight, we'll know the way. You see that as well as I do. May take a'day, a'year..." You kissed me, briefly and incredibly sweetly: a promise. "But, we'll know the way *home*, m'light... so, yeah, that means we have all the time in *every* world."

My hands closed over the fabric covering your breasts, where they somehow ended up when I'd melted. With that goofy smile across my lips, "Did you just say you're going to tell me what I hope you will?"

"Yeah." A smile quirked over your lips, too, "Might've."

"By the end of *this* night?"

"Will be at the front of your mind just as you wake up, yeah." Your lips met mine, kissing me slowly, and yet more sweetly. "Won't be able to forget a word I say."

"I *never* forget a word you say, Love." I narrowly avoided your next kiss, having it land just beside my lips when I tilted my head slightly away. But, you were of course undaunted, those lips trailing tenderly across my face, "So, y'know the sun's setting?"

That grunt, to say you definitely knew.

"Well, even with all the time in the world... She's still waiting."

Your kisses grew a hair more aggressive, urgent, with only a grunt in response. Traveling down my jawline as your hand tangled into my hair, tipping my head back.

I let you without the slightest complaint, even when I knew I shouldn't have.

Letting your lips dip further, to love my throat. Loving me enough that I was positive evidence would be left behind: that bruises shaped just like your beautiful mouth would appear on my skin. Kissing in a way that made my head instinctively tip back, cradled in your hand, giving you all the access you possibly wanted.

"Love…" My voice was air, losing all train of thought: the protest I had been about to make. Your kisses continuing slowly down my throat, to my shoulder, with your tongue perfectly soft against my skin trailing in the wake of your kiss. Following after you left your tender marks of love behind. Trailing slowly over my clavicle, into the sensitive hollow of my throat, dipping lower to the space between my breasts.

Making me forget my sister entirely.

"You know," One of my hands found the nape of your neck, my fingertips pushing into your hair, keeping you there. "I used to stare up at the moon, as a child, and think I saw you there. A knight on horseback, rearing up like he was about to jump off the moon and save me from my nightmares… Used to imagine I was Rapunzel, waiting for my knight to set me free from my tower."

I felt your lips quirk in a smile against me, kissing the swell of my breast, just over my pounding heart. "Yeah?"

"Mhm." I leant down to kiss the top of your head, staying there:

happily breathing only you. Saying something we have said even more than the previous conversation, and yet never tired of just the same. "And, since then, when I see our future I see our tree up on that hill... I'm always sitting in its shade, with you right beside me... surrounded by the magic of you and I."

"Magic of *only* us?" Your nose pushed aside the fabric covering me to reveal more of my skin. In a far too skilled way that let you easily free that breast entirely in the next kiss, drawing a gasp from my lips as you immediately found and took its peak. Speaking between loving me, "Sounds perfect, m'heart."

"It is... that's all I want. All I've ever needed... You're my past, present and future. You're my heart, spirit and my love. My everything."

You started kissing your way back up me, "That's a'lot a'things."

"Well, everything *is* a lot of things."

"Suppose it is." A laugh left you, one with *true* sound: a deep quake that made my eyes fall closed, that made my world tilt in harmony. As you drew just enough away to kiss my forehead, that beautiful sea in your eyes alight as if they were truly the stars. "Really don't know how I—"

I interrupted by kissing you softly and briefly, because I knew what you'd say: you really didn't know how you "deserved" me. I knew, because I always felt the same when I looked at you. Always wondering why the world chose *me* out of everyone else to be yours, what I had done to deserve *you*.

Why you chose to give your love to *me*.

"You were made for me, and I'm made for you. It's really as

simple as that, Love." I kissed you very slowly, tenderly, my eyes never once leaving yours. "And, Gods, my sweet Love, I do love *you*."

I let my arm wrap around you to hook under your shoulder, holding you close to me as my other hand pushed deeper into your hair to keep you where you were. Kissing you softly and sweetly at first, my tongue parting your lips gently to find your own. Our eyes closing only as we fell into that beautiful dance of our love... until both of your gentle hands found the side of my face. Drawing just enough away to speak, and no more, as those eyes saw *me*.

Your voice, that smooth thunder, rumbled through all of me, nearly making my eyes close again. "You do trust me, yeah?"

"Entirely. Of course... yes, I do." I didn't try to ease how breathless my voice was: how much I *do* trust you shining through every syllable, "You know that."

"Enough to make your sister wait... just a wee while longer?"

"Something tells me she won't have to wait at all. If time *is* yours."

"Ours." You drew just enough away to kiss the tip of my nose. Those beautiful eyes telling me every word you didn't know how to say aloud. "No, she won't."

"Which means she likely wasn't waiting at all... in her perception."

"Likely not even a moment."

"Then, yes. I'll gladly make her wait. But, just so you know, my Love..." My hands found either side of your face, kissing the tip of your nose as you had to mine. Making that beautiful, giant grin cross your face, "Even if she *did* have to wait, I'd still say 'yes' to whatever it is you're going to ask me."

That smile grew, crinkling those perfect eyes, "Yeah?"

"Absolutely."

"Then, you'll let me take you somewhere?" You quirked a brow, "Just one last little place, before we go and find your sister. And, probably have to… leave."

"What place?"

"That a 'yes'?" That brow lifted higher, the true hope in those eyes making a soft laugh leave my lips. "And, you'll follow me blindly?"

"Anywhere." I brushed your hair back, behind your ears, rising onto my toes to kiss you. Just once, and sweetly. "How long is it? From here, I mean."

You glanced at the softly snowing sky, "An hour, probably."

"Then, an hour and a half, to be safe. I do sometimes walk slow."

"Who said *you* had to walk it, too? It *is* my idea." You had me in your arms, tightly cradled to your chest, before you had even finished speaking. Moving so suddenly that I couldn't help the laugh from escaping my lips, my arms wrapping immediately around you, as they always do, as you didn't hesitate to start down that path.

It was truly two hours away, likely, at a normal speed…

But, you didn't *go* at said normal speed: making it down the narrow path the ridge turned into, leading to the road down below, and down to those magnificent hills in *less* than that projected hour.

I watched that beautiful landscape passing by us, contentedly in silence. Simply lost in a trance, listening to your walking and steady breaths. Mixing beautifully with the soft songs chirping out from the tall trees of the woods along the way, the gentle ringing melody of the birds celebrating the recent passing of a storm.

Peaceful, despite our fast pace.

Keeping my head resting happily against your shoulder most of that time, and my arms around you: with one looped loosely around your neck, as the other crossed over your chest and onto your opposite shoulder, with my hands holding one another. And, my eyes staying on the beautiful sight of your face, studying every detail of you as if you truly were a perfect work of art.

Because, to me, you really *are*.

We continued along that road until we came to a gathering of trees larger than the rest, thicker than the forest had been. One that made the path split suddenly into a new road going either left or right, as a dense, green wall that must have spanned hundreds of acres blocked the way forward: forming a beautiful barrier to what hid behind.

But, you went neither left nor right, not even slowing your stride as you started to break through that wall. Passing through the thick bushes and tree branches as though they didn't exist, letting nothing stop you from reaching what we knew was hidden on the other side. And, only slowing once you *did* break through to the land beyond: stopping entirely, actually, as soon as you cleared the wall, to let our eyes see the world around us, to see all the magnificence those trees protected.

How those beautiful woods fell away to reveal the miles of open, gently rolling hills: a sea of endless green as far as an eye can see. The rolling hills that I could stare at for the rest of my life, and likely never tire of, whose indescribable beauty truly seems impossible in any reality.

Impossible, and yet somehow *true*—in yours.

It was just a moment's glance before your eyes found mine... yet, it made your eyes dance with the most beautiful kind of pride. Leaning down to kiss me, long and sweet, as you freed my legs to stand on my own. Keeping my body with yours as you spoke: in a voice that was wonderfully husky, *proud*, "Welcome home, my beautiful wife... my Life."

"Likewise, my beautiful husband." I rose onto my toes to kiss you, short and sweet. Falling back down to my natural height as a giant smile spread across my face, as my sparkling eyes told you a thousand words without needing to say one aloud. Warning you of what I planned to do, before I'd actually do so: before I slipped easily from your arms and started to run, laughing as freely as I only can with you.

Knowing you'd catch me, when you laughed just the same.

You let me run for as long as I could without losing my breath. Several times acting as though you'd nearly caught me—letting your hand either barely catch my own, or slip around my waist before slipping back away—and then as if you'd lost your breath and fell behind again, letting me regain a small distance.

And, it was only as I crested a high hill that your arm came around my waist and truly caught me. Easily turning me around in that arm, to let your hands find either side of my waist just as my own found your shoulders. Lifting me from the ground as you spun us a few times, making me laugh again—bright and true, for you—before you let me fall against you. Into your chest, as your arms wrapped around my torso and mine did the same around your neck. Letting yourself tumble heavily down to the Earth; to let us both roll down that hill, wrapped around one another.

Just as we have all our lives.

Coming to a gentle stop at where that hill's bottom started to lift into the next gentle curve. Landing with me safely under you, as your lips took possession of mine, and I did the same to yours. Kissing me until we had to stop and find air: breathless from all that we had been doing to get there, the running, laughing and rolling.

Making you speak between heavy breaths, as those sparkling eyes showed me the world, "We aren't even there, yet, m'dear. And… can barely stand."

"Mm, but as you said: time is *yours*, my Love." My hands found either side of your perfect face, brushing your beautifully mussed and sweaty hair out from your eyes. My hands happily cradling that perfect face, "We can stay here forever, if you need to."

"W'could, sure. But… m'afraid I'm rather impatient t'show you." You kissed the tip of my nose, making that ridiculous grin cross my face. "It's just on the other side of the hill… *if* you want to see?"

"You know, too well, I'm far too curious to say 'no' to anything like that." I let my hands slide down from your face to find your either breast, gently pushing against you—since we both knew I wouldn't get anywhere, unless you moved on your own, first.

You rolled off of me the moment I asked it, hopping to your feet before I could rise on my own. Just to hold a hand down to me, and help me return to your side. Leading us much slower up the next hill, to stop right at its uppermost point, and let me see the sight that waited below.

To where the hills flattened for a little while, making space for a little calm creak to cut gently through the green: and, making room for one little building to stand in the otherwise open land, just beyond the edge of that little creak. A little building that had appeared in many perfect places throughout our dreams, ever since I was fifteen, but I hadn't seen in quite a long time.

My hand—the one without its arm wrapped around your waist, to hold onto your belt, as your own arm was draped over my shoulders—came to rest over your perfect heart, my eyes lifting from the sight to find yours, "How?"

"Same as everything in this world's come to exist, m'Danie." You leant down to kiss me, just once but slowly and tenderly. Speaking against me, "For *you*, my Love."

You guided our way to that perfect little building, slowly: lost in a beautiful trance. As we talked both about nothing and everything at once, strolling as though we truly had all the time in the world. Because we did, in our land blanketed by the bright stars shining in the night's sky; our land healing, under a layer of pure white, soft snow.

A perfect world, guided by the simplicity of being alone—*with you*.

We travelled to where that perfect little shed waited. The one that had been filled by tools and storage, a workshop of a sort, when I first saw it so long ago. Until, you had moved all that was once in the front further back one night when I was fifteen, nearly sixteen: I don't know when or how you did, I just know I saw it as it had first been that one night, and then several nights later… came back to find it as it still was now.

Grand in a simple way, as everything you decorate is.

The magical little room was made entirely out of rough wood: of wide planks cut to precisely the same width, their grains lined neatly up with the next as if it were all still one tree. With, ever since the night when it first changed, enough space for a double mattress and little else, still covered in an old plaid comforter and two pillows.

Barely enough room: the top of that mattress was pushed against the wall, partly beneath old shelving that was thankfully high enough to not hit our heads when we were in that bed, but close to doing so; its bottom butted-up against a work-table whose surface had been cleared since said night to hold many candles, surely at least a dozen and a half, and a small radio. With its one side two feet away from the doors, and the other against crates and storage boxes that formed a sort of wall.

A "wall" that was covered strategically by a white sheet, matching another sloping gracefully between the rafters overhead, seamlessly blending as one: as if the mattress were surrounded by a canopy. As if it were under a gently rippling sky of clouds, I've always thought, shifting in the little air making its way through gaps between the roof and walls.

Those rafters above were also strung with soft white lights, I can't possibly forget to mention that, such as from Christmas: wrapped just so around the shelves and table, draped over that wall of boxes, to cast their glow over the space, to dance along with the orange flames of those candles. Turning a simple shed into something that looked as though it had jumped out of a fairytale… or at least, it appeared to be so, to me.

My lips silently parted as my feet landed on the well-worn floors, my eyes lifting to see the inside: pure wonder, and awe, washing over every part of me. It was dark—despite my own still glowing personal light around me—since the sun had a while before set below the mountains, but slowly started to flicker into life as you lit one of those many candles, casting a perfect orangish glow over the room. Carefully lighting the rest as I stepped fully inside.

Or, as far as I could without the edge of that bed hitting my calves.

A wide smile crossed my lips when my eyes met yours, entirely showcasing all of my awe: and not just wonderment caused by the room, but as you should really expect by now, by *you*. "I didn't know this was still here."

"'Course it is." You pushed the doors closed, sliding its many locks in place. Those old floors strangely comfortingly creaking under your weight as you moved, as you turned back to find where I stood once you were sure it was secure. Though, not really having to move at all to be right behind me. "M'fond a'this place. For some reason."

"Hm… so am I." My smile grew to that likely goofy state, "Odd coincidence."

"Very strange." Your arms wrapped slowly around my waist, drawing my back to your chest. Your lips tenderly finding the side of my throat as you spoke, kissing softly. Making my head instinctively tip the other way as you did, giving you as much access as you wanted, my body leaning into yours. "Maybe we can find out why."

"Mm, maybe." My voice was already breathless, my eyes struggling to stay open as you slowly, skillfully, kissed your way down my throat. My arms wrapping around my waist to find your hands, entwining our fingers as my head tipped back, onto your shoulder. "Might be a mystery we can't solve."

You grunted, "Can solve *any* mystery."

"Oh?"

"Sure. I've magic powers…" You kissed just *so*. Drawing a content moan from me, as my hands tightened around yours. "See? *Magic*."

"Mhm, definitely magic." My voice barely carried sound, my body melting freely into yours: letting your arms alone hold my weight. "My Love…"

"I know, m'light." Your beautiful voice rumbled through me, lowered and drawn out in *that* way, drawing another happy moan from me as one of your hands slipped free of mine: letting your palm glide up the fabric covering my torso, and over the soft swells of my breasts. Finding the ties of my dress, and starting to gently tug its ribbon free, as your lips trailed achingly slowly down my neck.

Making my head tip even further back onto you, rising slightly onto my toes.

You spoke against me in that magnificent way, with every slow word a kiss, "Want t'show y'how much I love you, before we go. If that's alright with you."

Your name left my lips: the best word in my whole world. As one of my freed hands fell from my waist to find your thigh, its fingers closing around the jeans covering you as you pulled the first cross of my ribbon loose.

Your fingertips deliberately brushing my skin as you slowly lowered to find the next, letting the fabric part to showcase my cleavage as your hand slid down to flatten over my stomach. Covering all of me: with your thumb below my breasts, and your three middle fingers splayed across my belly; with your strong fingertips pressing into the side of my waist and between my ribs just *so*, in a truly magical way I can't explain; as your pinkie reached down to *that* part of me, just where the bodice of my dress ended, letting it slowly slip through the bottom crossing of ribbon, gently tugging to test what you wanted.

My hand uncrossed from over my waist as the other released its hold on your jeans, knowing what you wanted and telling you that you may. So that, when you pulled the ribbon entirely free in a smooth and quick tug, my dress slipped easily from my body, puddling around our feet just as you'd wanted.

Letting you draw my back tighter against you, until my body was fully against you, as your lips trailed tenderly across my shoulder. Your hands slowly sliding to either of my hips, asking me to turn in your arms, and I just as slowly did: getting your perfect smile to lazily cross your lips, beautifully.

The most beautiful sight in my world.

My hands found your either breast, leaning my torso slightly away from you to let your eyes dip lower than my face, to admire all of me. Waiting for those eyes to return to mine before I let my breasts barely come back to yours, strategically so: before my lips found beside yours, feathering over them as I spoke. "I'm *yours*, my Love."

Your perfect fingertips brushed slowly up my spine to find the nape of my neck, angling my head back to kiss me, truly unspeakably passionately. As my hands slid slowly down your stomach from your breasts to find the hem of your shirt, lifting it over your head to throw aside. Hearing the fabric hit the wall with a soft slap that briefly took my eyes from yours, my breaths freezing.

Until your gentle hand found the side of my face to bring my gaze back onto you: onto those eyes that really do shine like the stars. Letting your thumb sweep tenderly across my cheekbone, as my lips slowly, softly started to feather over your chest, and between your breasts. Loving every exposed inch of you that I could. As my hands slid back down from your shoulders to caress where I'd kissed, moving *very* slowly. My gentle fingertips trailing softly down your stomach to find your belt, letting one hand's fingers dip between your waistband and warm skin. A touch that made your pelvis instinctively come closer to me: that made a low, deep sound rumble through you.

Letting my lips travel slowly, delicately across your chest, through the soft hair that covered you, before I rose onto my toes; letting my kiss trail over your collar-bone, your throat, across your jawline and chin, pulling away just shy of meeting your lips as I let my hand gently tug that belt free. As I easily undid the button and zipper standing in the way with my thumb. My eyes finding yours, as those jeans fell down to find my lost dress. Watching that sea react to me as my hand lovingly found that sacred part of you, sending another deep sound rumbling through you.

"I love you." My breaths flowed heavily enough to blow the soft hair hanging around your face, yet my words barely carried sound: they didn't *need* to make sound, when my eyes said everything. "Only, and *all* of you, my Love. Always."

Your hands found either side of my face, leaning your forehead against my own to let your eyes see right into mine: telling me far more than words will ever have the power to say.

Making the beautiful words you *did* say mean all the more to me.

"I love *you*. Only, and *all* of *you*, my Life... Forever." Your lips gently parted mine to let our tongues entwine: a kiss that made the whole world tilt around us, my hands finding either of your shoulders to stay standing. Your own leaving the side of my face as my knees gave way, and easily lifting me—letting my legs wrap around your waist, my arms doing the same around your throat to hold you close to me, my hands vanishing into your beautiful hair.

Giving you all I had, as you gave me all *you* had: as you, my Love, filled all of me with your divine love as soon as my body was against yours, pulling a sharp, surprised gasp from my lips. A gasp followed by a *very* happy moan. You caught the soft sound with that kiss, becoming deeper, stronger, even more passionate than before.

Even when that shouldn't have been possible.

Stepping forward to lower us to that mattress as that kiss deepened. As we moved as one. And, perhaps it was the kiss that made you forget where it was in that room, exactly, or the fact that we were so far into one another that all other thought of what was around us simply escaped our minds. But, whatever happened, the mattress was closer than you either thought or remembered, if you'd given it any thought at all.

All I know is that you took a step forward, and we fell to that bed, *fast*.

You caught us with your knees and one of your hands, taking all of the fall onto yourself: my back barely even made contact to that mattress, until *after* you had landed safely there. And, my only reaction was a gasp at the rate we fell, at how you were in fact one with me as we did, coming even *more* to me in a way that was far from bad.

But, you pulled away from that magnificent kiss as soon as my back was against the bed, your eyes studying every inch of my face, sincerely worried, "I hurt you?"

"No." A laugh left me, the one you love: a sound that made that magnificent smile cross your face, crinkling your beautiful eyes. As I kissed you, slowly and deeply. My hand finding the side of your perfect face to brush some of your hair from your eyes as I drew away to meet them, "No, Love. I'm perfect. Absolutely, entirely perfect."

"Yeah." You kissed my nose, that smile growing. "You *are* that, m'light."

"Likewise, my knight." I drew you back into our previously interrupted kiss. My hand leaving your face to slide around your waist, finding your behind as my hips rose to find yours: asking you to take all I had to give.

And, you, my beautiful magnificent husband, you gave me every last piece of yourself in return. Taking us far beyond the stars, into the land that exists beyond most humans' comprehension—though, what's quite possibly the only beautiful world that we, you and I, are truly meant to live within…

The world of true *Love, Love.*

Our world cradled us softly, gently, perfectly, until I'd given you all the energy I had, and you had given me the same—until, we both knew *morning* was dawning.

In the reality that we always do have to return to.

You knew it first, that our time was waning, and knew we could no longer fight it: no matter *how* desperately we wanted to. Forcing your mind to focus on the thoughts of what we had to do, before that little time ran out, and how to make it all possible, before it would be too late. But, even when that beautiful mind was acutely aware of every second that passed us by, you didn't rush *my* slower mind. Letting me drift in an almost sleep-like trance for as long as possible.

Utterly calm, and peaceful, as I always am when I'm aware of *only* you.

Not of time, or space, but vividly conscious of your hand as it lifted from the back of my neck, away from where my face was nestled against your chest, to gently brush my hair out from my face and tuck it tenderly behind my ear. Making time and space lose all meaning to me, as those perfect eyes studied me, all of me, as if it may be the last time you'd be able to: because, you knew our last glimpse of this night was nearly gone, and the time to wake was close.

And, when you spoke—your perfect voice rumbling through all of me, just like thunder before a beautiful storm—I truly lost every worry or care about anything in the world, *any* world or reality: except for *you*, my Love. *Truly*, only you. "Think it's time t'find your sister, my light."

I moaned, refusing to leave that light sleep… because, I knew that would mean soon having to leave you, and I never want to do any such thing.

But, we both knew what needed to happen: making a heavier breath run through you, your arm loosening around my waist to flatten its palm across my back, rubbing in those gentle circles to "wake" me. Because, you knew it always worked, and that it also *does* have the power to calm me as nothing else can. You've always known that better than anyone. In a few seconds my hand closed, slowly, making my nails drag through the soft hair over your chest, just in front of my face. As my legs curled further over you, holding my body closer to yours.

Something which should have been impossible, when I was *on* you.

My eyes heavily, slowly, blinking open as a groan ran softly through me. As one of my legs uncurled to stretch down the length of yours, with my foot ending just on top of yours. Letting that hand slide from your chest to find the side of your waist while my leg stretched; while the other hand pushed through the blankets covering me to find yours at my waist, entwining our fingers. Sleepily tilting my head back against your shoulder to meet your eyes, after my long waking process, with a smile already across my kiss-plumped lips.

Because, there will never be a time when the sight of you isn't my everything.

That perfect smile crossed your lips, lazily from your own lingering tiredness. As your hand gently found the side of my face, your thumb sweeping tenderly across my cheek. A small thing that made my grin grow, "Hey, you."

"Hi, *you.*" I turned to kiss the inside of your wrist, my eyes staying solely on yours: letting both our smiles grow into goofy proportions. With yours quirking yet higher as I turned my face against you, when I yawned. "What time's it now?"

You tenderly kissed the top of my head, your perfect smile beautifully crinkling the skin around your perfect eyes. "Doesn't matter."

"Mm…" My hand slid back up your chest to find one of your shoulders: you knew what I wanted, sliding your own further around my waist to draw me up to reach the level of your face. Letting me kiss the tip of your nose, "But, y'said we should go?"

"Sure." You kissed just to the side of my lips, watching my smile grow as you started to do the same to the rest of my face, speaking between kissing. Your free hand finding the nape of my neck as you did, tangling back into my hair to keep me there. "But, the world can wait, 'til whenever you're ready to."

"Mm…" I tilted my face to the side, letting you find the underside of my jaw. "But, what if I never will be?"

You made that perfect grunt, "Aren't you?"

"For what will follow, undoubtedly. But… I don't want to leave you."

"You won't." Your lips found mine, kissing slowly and deeply, as you always perfectly do. Letting your eyes come back to me, pulling away from that kiss only as you slowly turned to shift me from on top of you. To be *under* you, instead. "You never *do* or *have*… or *will* leave my side, m'light. You know that."

"And, I know we have to wake from *here*, in order to find our way home in every world…" I kissed your nose, "But, that doesn't make it any easier, does it?"

"Never." You kissed me just as perfectly the same again, before reluctantly pulling away. Meeting my eyes, tenderly, "So, come find home with me, my light."

You kissed my nose before you swung your legs from the bed, and rose. Doing so before you could talk yourself out of it, before either of us could. And, I sat up as you did: pulling the blankets around my shoulders, and yawning into them, as you started to search for your jeans.

Watching you openly, since you definitely don't mind when I do.

"We've already found it." I spoke as you knelt to search under the table, not finding what you sought: it was one of those instances where something important vanishes in a sudden and unreasonable way, for seemingly no reason.

Because, there's *always* a reason.

You peeked only your eyes over the foot of the bed, in a way that —as you'd known it would—drew a laugh from my lips: with one of your brows quirked even though we both knew that *you* knew the answer full well, "Found what?"

"Home." My smile grew at the sight of undeniably hopeful happiness in your eyes. Because, you knew what I was saying, beyond my words: *my* eyes left no doubt. We both knew that to fully jump to my true home, to you, I'd have to make a choice to leave my other home behind. And, I had never been able to—being unable to afford it on my own was the biggest reason: I would've found you at once, no matter what, had I been able to. But, the other reason, was because I'd always feared leaving my family, even as I knew they would be fine… and I know you need me far, far more. "I don't have to find what's right here, where *you* are, my Home."

You rose back to your full magnificent height, giving up on that search, "What ever happened t'your worry about your sister?"

My smile grew ridiculously, "You."

"Me?" Your brows both rose higher, as if you didn't know: as you said just what *I* had said at the quarry. "Whatever did *I* do?"

"Now, *that's* a list too long to name."

You stepped one foot onto the mattress, one brow lowering, "Is it, then?"

"It is… and, thankfully, you already know every word."

"Do I?"

A soft laugh left me, "You know *everything*, my Love."

"You mean," the other brow lowered, as your lips rose, "*Your* everything?"

"I mean, *you,* my everything." You came back to me when I stood. Making it to my feet, clumsily, as you stepped fully onto the mattress to catch me before I lost balance: as I undoubtedly would have, if you hadn't caught me. If you hadn't drawn me safely against you, as I let my body melt back against yours, my eyes falling closed. "*You*, my Love, are what happened to my worry for Katie, or anything else: because, I've selfishly realized I'm only worried about *my* life now... about you. Is that alright?"

You grunted, the smiling grunt, "Undoubtedly."

"And, if I can't stand being *without* you anymore?"

"I'd only say 'likewise,' my Life."

"Which would probably make her happy, too. Wouldn't it?" I spoke in a very happy sigh, making an equally content, deep breath run through you as I tenderly kissed your chest. My arms wrapping around your waist to hold my own torso against yours. "My sister, I mean. She'd be happy to know... I don't even know how to say it, really."

You kissed the top of my head. Already knowing I was about to unleash a flood of words on you, as soon as you set them free by simply saying, "Yeah?"

I spoke at that incredibly fast rate which only you are able to follow, as you always do: following my words without interrupting, and listening to every word, as only you truly do, "She says I don't have to worry about her... that I should only think about myself, and get to you. So, she'd be happy t'know I *can't* worry: now I *only* see you, and *can't* spend another moment without you... I mean, I've always felt that way, of course. But, let myself think it's selfish to focus on what *I* want... even if I know they'll be happy if *I* am, in my head it's never added up that way, since I have to leave *them* to... but, well, I realized it doesn't matter: I really don't *care* how selfish, or how crazy it'll make me look... *You* are everything, and I *need* you in my life, to be happy, to be myself. And, I—is that okay?"

"Might just be I'm sharing a similarly selfish mind," You waited for my eyes to lift up to yours. Your lips twitching higher as you tugged the comforter back over my shoulders, only still around me because you'd caught it as I fell into you. "But, I don't find thinking entirely about someone *else* selfish, m'dear."

"So, it's okay?"

"Undoubtedly."

"And, when we leave here..." I leant forward, rising onto my toes, to let my chin rest against yours. A heavy, and very happy, breath flowing through me: a breath filled entirely by the magnificent scent of you, "We'll start finding our way... *there*, yeah?"

"Soon as possible, yeah."

"I just wish we could stay here... until we have to go."

You grunted, "Me, too."

"We can't?"

"You wouldn't forgive yourself for not making sure she's fine. Even if we both know she is." One of your hands gently found the side of my face, to meet my eyes somehow even more sincerely. Your smile lifting higher on one side, to expose a perfect canine, "But, *after* we do, promise me you'll trust that feeling, in the future. Trust she's fine... and come to me. Yeah?"

"I promise you just that, my Love, and more." I let my lips find yours, sweetly and softly, yet briefly. "I *can*, now that I've also realized, because I do trust *you* entirely... surely, that means I should start trusting myself, too."

"Surely. As much as *I* trust you." You leant down to rest your forehead against my own, "You've never let me down… or your sister. Have you?"

"Haven't I?"

Your perfect nose nudged mine, "Not once, no."

"Then, if you—" A surprised gasp escaped me when you interrupted, surprised as I really shouldn't have been. Kissing me deeply, tenderly, as your hand tangled into my knotted hair to gently tilt my head back: to take all you possibly could from that kiss. So entirely, that I had to be the one who pulled away, all of my breaths gone, "Alright, then… as much as I don't want to… you know where we have to go?"

Your lips feathered over my face, smiling as you kissed me, "The sea."

"Right," I tilted my head back as your lips trailed down to find my throat, as your body folded around mine. And, I spoke like air, "Seems a bit broad, doesn't it?"

"Undoubtedly… will ask around."

"Ask who?"

"Someone—anyone who may've seen her."

"Alright." I kissed you one more time, avoiding when you tried to kiss me again. Knowing we'd never go, otherwise. Slipping easily out of your arms, when it should have been impossible, and taking a small step back. My eyes tightening when I saw the exaggerated pout over your face. "Hey, it's *your* idea."

"Doesn't mean I like the details of *my* idea."

"Could you," I pointed, "hand me that, anyway?"

"Sure… But, only since I have to." You released an over-dramatic sigh, bending to retrieve my dress from where it had fallen to the floor. Helping me get it back into its place, before we resumed the search for your lost jeans. But, still, between the two of us all we could find was your shirt, and your boots.

Eventually, I realized why.

"They're gone, Love." I rose from searching under the bed you were lifting, kissing you on the cheek before crossing to unlatch the doors. Only pausing when you caught one of my hands, stopping me before I could go: but, I wasn't going to without you, anyways. "It only leaves one thing."

"It does." Your smile lifted into its full magnificence. Your eyes tightening on mine, even as your smile stayed in place, because we both already knew *nothing* could part us. "I'm jus' coming with you, if that's alright. Not letting you leave my sight."

"Quite alright with me." I rose to kiss your cheek again as you pulled the door open, stepping outside together. "You didn't *really* think I would, right?"

"No." You kissed my forehead, as we walked to where we both had known Silence would be waiting for us: drinking patiently from the creak. "But, panicked nonetheless."

Right… because we're both a wee bit protective, aren't we?

And, that's why I happily stayed just on the other side of the horse, well within one another's sight, as you went about your business: busying myself, at first, by at least attempting to tame my wild hair, before I simply settled for standing beside Silence, calmly petting his nose as I waited.

Thanking the horse for all he had done for us that night.

Only letting my eyes truly rise to find you when you stepped to my side, without a word. Keeping your eyes away from mine, focused on fiddling with the reigns, as my eyes freely studied you: keeping your eyes away for just long enough to let me take in what covered you, and admit what it undoubtedly meant, before you looked at me.

And, let those proud eyes take all breath from me...

Because, *all* of you shone with the greatest sort of pride: seeming to stand taller than before, your strong shoulders squared, and your chin tilted higher. With the only thing remaining from before being your boots, with your calves now bare and showcased under the heavy woolen blanket: the plaid with its many perfect shades of greens, browns and blue, falling just below your knees and hanging longer in the back to nearly touch your ankles. Belted at your hips with possibly the same belt of before, but now carrying a leather sporran at the center; with its front stamped with a symbol for our tree, outlined in runes. And, a matching sheathe hung low on your hip to hold your blade.

If one hadn't known before, you'd never doubt what you are at the sight: and, that was why it had been exactly what you had worn the night when you'd told me that much of your whereabouts. What you have ended up wearing every night you share something groundbreaking.

When you *do* something truly extraordinary.

A sight that I always, undoubtedly, appreciate for obvious reasons even beyond that knowledge, which I don't believe I need to name: reasons most women, at least, will understand.

You barely turned away from the horse, barely met my eyes for a second, before I closed the short distance between us. Coming right into your side—returning to where I belong—my arm slipping around your waist as yours did the same to mine. As your other hand gently found the side of my face to draw me higher onto my toes as you came down to me, kissing me in that way which would make one think we hadn't seen one another in years not seconds. Letting a smile return to my lips once I had slowly returned to my height, my eyes telling you every last thought I held without the need of words, as our eyes always do.

We only do ever use words to truly hear the other's voice.

Which you did, as your lips quirked higher. That hand lifting to softly tug on one of my new pigtails. Speaking softly, and blowing your beautifully hot breath lightly over my face, as you twisted my hair delicately around your fingertips: amazed by the sight and simply by me, just as I was amazed by all of you. "Like your hair this way."

"Like *you* this way." I rose briefly back onto my toes, to quickly but tenderly kiss your cheek. Dropping back to my natural height as I spoke, my words barely audible, "I mean… obviously, I love you absolutely *every* way. But, it definitely doesn't hurt anything."

"Obviously." You leant down to kiss my forehead, as tenderly as I had your cheek. Twisting my pigtail a couple more times around your fingers; drawing that laugh from me as you gently tugged it, tilting my head back to sweetly kiss me. "Good thing, too. Would be a problem, if y'found me repulsive."

I softly laughed, again, "Oh?"

"Yeah… since I plan t'marry you, fast as I can find you."

"Even if my parents won't love that plan, quite as much as I do?" I laughed again, this time with a light snort, when you scrunched up your face as if the thought stunk. Declaring how little you cared about that possibility. "Won't stop us, of course… they realize we won't have a *traditional* relationship. But, still don't think they'll be happy with us getting married in under a month."

"*Month*?" You lifted your brows, drawing me closer to Silence's side instead of his nose: preparing to be on our way. "Was thinking less than a'week, m'self."

"I said '*under*' a month, didn't I?"

"*Far* under, yeah." You kissed my forehead, tenderly. "If you'll have me?"

I kissed your chin, my grin absolutely ridiculous, "Obviously, yes."

"Right then, we will immediately. After all, s'only your father who's not fond a'me, yeah?" Again, you slightly scrunched your face, but this time at a painful memory. "Remember when he walked in on us, first he met me… caught us—"

"Talking, just talking."

"Sure. Have a'lot t'say." Your smile grew when I laughed, "Recall a'comment 'bout him disliking my 'smirk,' before his fist met m'face." You winked, in that magic way, "Was worth it, of course. But, not really a sign of him *liking* my face."

"Your *nose*, actually." My hand lifted to find the side of your face, to let a fingertip tap the tip of said nose, getting your lips to twitch higher. "Really made me mad."

"Sure. Nose brutality should be a'crime."

"Really, it should be."

You winked again, and just as perfectly, "Luckily, your mother'll balance his thoughts. Will like me jus' for loving, and caring for you. Yeah?"

"As will my dad, even if he won't admit it."

"Right. Which brings us back to the certainty of a week, eh?"

"Sure. So long as you're prepared for… all that."

"M'prepared for *you*." You softly kissed my forehead, your eyes leaving mine only to swing onto the horse's back. Holding one of your hands instantly down to me, with that magnificent smile of yours, "That's all I know, m'life."

"Then, you better show me how to truly get to you. Hm?" I took your hand the moment you offered it: resting my foot over yours to use it as a stirrup, to safely swing onto the horse's back behind you. My arms wrapping around your waist, and my chin finding your shoulder, "Will you?"

"Will show you everything." Your smile twitched into its full, and perfect glory. Gently urging Silence forward: moving much slower than we had to for just a little while more, because you had more to say before we made it to the town; before we'd reach what'd make us soon wake. "But, I've a strange sense that you, my Life, already know all of that. Don't you?"

"Perhaps. But, I have a strange sense you'll show me anyway, my Love."

You made that smiling grunt, "Do you?"

"Undoubtedly. Since I'll still want you to, no matter if I know already."

"And, you think *I* would do something purely because *you* want it?"

"Mhm." I kissed the side of your throat, "Anything I ask."

"And, anytime." You turned to kiss my forehead, tenderly of course, as one of your hands found mine at your waist, entwining our fingers. Keeping your lips on my skin as you spoke. "I just wish I knew what *one* right thing I did, that allowed *me* t'be the one to show you everything you ask... whatever brought me you."

"You're *you*, my Love."

"I am that. And, you make me grateful for it." Your lips found mine, kissing me just once: and magnificently. "Thank you, my Life... for everything."

"Sure thing." I squeezed your hand, giving you the wide smile that you would do anything to create. "Thank you, too, my Love... for everything."

"Sure thing." Your smile grew to expose both canines, the absolutely perfect smile that always makes my world tilt on its axis. Kissing my forehead once more, tenderly in ways beyond words, and lingering as your eyes fell closed—because, we both knew our dream was, then, truly starting to end.

And, well, that everything else would soon start to fall into place.

The best possible place to find someone who may have noticed my sister pass through the world, and where she might have gone, resided at the edge of a quiet little village. Which, to me, has always seemed as if from a movie: too perfect and peaceful to be true—yet was, in some form.

A village that I've roamed through far too many times to count throughout the years, and that I'm likely more familiar with than the town *I* live in. Because, each and every last building has meaning, to *us*; a memory where something important has happened at some point in our dreams.

It's little more than a few streets—winding, curving gravel roads more suited for people on foot and horses rather than vehicles—lined by beautiful little stone buildings. Mostly businesses, but also a few stray homes, and a single small hotel that I wouldn't have even known *was* one without a sign to say so, blending right into the rest. With a single pub resting on one edge of town; and, a simple yet absolutely beautiful old church on the outskirts of the other, connected to a quiet graveyard marked with incredibly old headstones.

The best sort of little village, is really all I can say.

Resting within a safe inlet where the hills lead down to the water, and the tall mountains in the distance sloped down to the sea, hooking around the bay. Where a couple of stone jetties reached out from the shore, to protect the boats docked there. Truly… just an unbelievably picturesque sight.

We had travelled along the main road from the hills to get there, likely half an hour away from where we had been, and only paid attention to the single building we had come to find. Drawing Silence up to the little parks where cars were meant to be, and some just then were, parallel parked.

I stood in the middle of that little old road, as you hitched Silence to some sort of a sign. My eyes studying the beautiful world around us while I still could, while I had a moment to, noting every last detail I could find: I knew the smallest thing could be what would tell me where this was in the waking reality, what would help me find you the moment I *did* wake… no matter how long it took to truly get there. Looking at the world in a way that I never had before, seeing everything, until you came back to my side.

Winking at me in that magic way of yours as you caught my hand, to lead us toward the pub, "You ready, then, my light?"

"As I can be." I bumped my arm gently into yours, perfectly matching your stride as we scaled the three steps leading from the street to the building's doors. "You?"

"As I can be." Your smile grew. Bumping me back, in a way that made a matching smile cross my face, as you shouldered the door open: and, well, as soon we crossed its threshold I was more than glad we'd taken a calm moment outside, a cringe taking place of that smile. Stepping into the chaos of many people who all spoke at once, and who were undeniably in some state of being drunk.

Of course, crowds are my enemy even on a good day: that's something most everyone who knows me is aware of, thanks to my eyes seeing much more than the average eye can. And, it's an enemy that has overwhelmed me constantly, nearly every day, without you at my side—without you, my tether, keeping me grounded, safe at your side.

And, well… that was *very* true in that pub.

Whose building, I'll detail real quick, is beautiful in a rough, worn-down, and old sort of way. Its ceilings rising high above, forming a sloping arch, its bowing support beams exposed and overhung by cobwebs. Both walls and floors made of wood that'd likely splinter bare-feet, lightened from many boots scuffing its top layer, worn down in clear paths from the tables to the bar. With those tables just at the edges of the room, to the left and the back, and the busy bar to the right.

And, the rest of the space filled entirely by bodies.

I would have surely lost all my senses, if not for you, within a second of being surrounded by their roaring noise, and high energy. If you hadn't steered us safely around all of the pushy bodies bumping into each other as they fought around the space, as they tried to talk to everyone and get to the bar at once. If *you* hadn't been there to buffer me from that crowd—if your mind didn't tune out all of that sound, and energy, so I wouldn't have to be touched by anyone living or otherwise, by any except you, I would've been lost.

But… I'm generally lost without you in any situation.

So, I stayed tightly at your side, as I do prefer to be. Staying in the one place I could be assured I wouldn't get bumped into by anyone else. My hand securely in yours, and the other clinging to the crook of your elbow, holding you as the lifeline you truly are, as my strides kept up with yours almost robotically. Never letting my eyes stray for more than a second before they'd flick back up to you: even as I tried to take in that building it was never for more than a moment, to ensure you were still at my side. As if someone else could have snuck their arm in your place as I looked away. And, constantly flicking my gaze to the ground between doing so, watching where I put my feet on the wood: since, it was terribly slick from alcohol being spilled in conversations.

Something that would have completely upset my balance—that slipperiness—if you weren't with me, and prepared to catch me when I *did* slip. Falling into you the most seriously just as you fought our way to the bar, making me lean heavily into your side as you leant across said bar to yell our question to the man behind it.

I didn't catch exactly what he'd said—despite easily hearing your every word: but, I suppose, that isn't surprising—before you started to lead us back through the crowd, and out the doors. I only learned what that man said once we were outside, and following those words. When you told me how he had, in fact, noticed a young woman of my sister's description pass through the town on a horse that was also as described, heading in the direction of the water. And, he'd seen her fly by on said horse just as he got there, likely a half hour before you asked.

But, when we made it down to the bay—and you asked a fisherman, who you actually know, the very same question—we learned she *had* indeed come there, but hadn't stayed for more than a moment, to ask after *us*, before she was gone again.

And, no... he didn't know where to.

We learned *that* on our own after we had walked along those jetties, talking to ourselves about where she may have possibly gone to. Walking slowly, lost in an undeniable calm, and peaceful trance, despite the time ticking quickly by us. Our steps leading us back to the beginning of a jetty, where a small building—a little workshop of sorts, for fishermen, though I'm afraid I don't know the true technical name—let that jetty become a rounded "deck." Making our way to where it started to bend around to overlook that perfect bay, before pausing to talk and think.

Though, both are very much the same: talking and thinking.

The view beyond was incredible. And, like most in our world, one I could spend hours studying, days, even years, without boring of the sight. The quiet blue bay stretching calmly out in the distance, before opening out to the sea. With the sharp shadows of the tall mountains rising high around the rounded bay, hazy silhouettes through the still snowy sky, casting graceful shadows in the water. As soft, gentle waves travelled slowly over its crystalline surface: creating a tranquil melody that could ease any mind. As the moon, shining and full, clear enough that I could see the shadow of the knight riding that rearing horse, sent its rays down to sparkle off that water… just like your eyes. Appearing more like a painting than anything real, but I knew it really was, of course.

Somewhere, in your reality.

We let our whole world become the soft sound of the water, and the rhythmic little squeak of an old swing-bench as it shifted in the breeze, hanging just outside the door of that workshop to overlook the view of that bay. Feeling the cool, gentle wind against our skin, listening just in case it had something to say, any warning or advice for our ears to hear; letting what we knew was about to happen fall away to simply *be*.

To simply feel the calm of the Earth, and focus on *hope*.

Until, I felt the weight of eyes watching me from afar: so afar, they weren't near enough to truly *see* me, except as a vision through a meditative mind. Until, I heard the soft whisper of my name traveling on the wind, to find me: in the voice of my sister, carried from likely a mile away from where *we* stood.

Making my eyes lift up to the magnificent mountains, where the bay narrowed for the sea, letting my sight extend far beyond what my *eyes* saw. Reaching all the way out to the distant cliff-sides; seeing as if I were on a ship in that sea, looking up to those high cliffs above.

To the beautiful sight that was undeniably my sister.

Her aura alone—the color of the Caribbean Sea—billowing out around her like giant wings, would have made it impossible to deny it was her. But, I would have known it was, even without that, simply by the *feeling* of her. She stood at the edge of the bluff, the sudden plateau at the end of our world, staring down to see where I truly was just as I somehow looked up at her, unmoving: there was no doubt that she *was* staring at me, even had I not felt her eyes. With her beautiful hair blowing impossibly perfectly out to her side... with all of her dressed in soft white, standing amidst the falling snow as if in a circle of her inner purity, blending right *into* the snow like a breathtaking portrait.

One with nature, and a Goddess of the elements, if ever there was.

She met my eyes for what was surely just a brief moment, but time seemed to slow around us, as the world seemed to zoom right in to where she was. So close, I swear I saw her smile down at me, at *us*, before she started to back away from the cliff's edge, slowly and gracefully like the wind. Hearing her words brushing over my ears as my beautiful sister vanished from sight, just as quickly as she appeared.

She said only two short sentences, but those sentences had the power to take away what fear I had left: to let me know that she really *was* okay, and would stay so. She said, "Go find your freedom, Dan. I'll be alright."

And, then… we did just that.

We traveled calmly, slowly, knowing we no longer had to rush.

Our horse carrying us from that bay all the way up to the beautiful untouched world beyond: neither of us saying a word as we travelled, not daring to break the beautiful silence, the peace, enveloping us. We simply lived entirely in each other's eyes, as we made our way to where we were meant to be.

To the plateau at the end of our world.

Finding what we needed in the form of an old wooden door, free-standing at the cliff's furthest edge. Where there was nothing to see behind it, but open dark sea. A door that looked as though it belonged in a fairytale: with its top softly rounded, its grains deep and well-defined; its old door knob intricate and long.

A door I had seen several times before… in visions when alone.

I was off the horse as soon as my eyes found the sight. With you, my Love, at my side since we truly did refuse to ever part again. Letting our boots land heavily on the Earth, on the soft snow, to slowly close the short distance to that door.

Stopping only once we were a couple feet away, just near enough to read the paper stuck—with blue-tape, which left no doubt to who left it: that *is* a trademark of my sister—right at its center, waiting to be found. Reading its words easily, even at a distance, because we already knew what it said: *the key isn't to unlock a door, but unlock a heart and set the love inside free*—so, be free, Dan... be *with* him."

"I've seen this before..." My voice was barely audible, but of course you heard me, even when we stood in rather strong wind. "What'll happen when we open the door."

"Yeah," You squeezed my hand, speaking just as softly. "Me, too."

I took a single step closer, knowing we had to. And, you came right along with me, "If we walk through, we'll truly find *our* world, won't we? I mean, *this* one... just without anything bad. We'll see..."

You waited for my words to trail away, before finishing for me, "We'll see how it's always been. Without our worry standing in the way."

"And, just *us*." I took another small step closer. And, of course, you did just the same, as my eyes lifted up to find yours. "That's why she was here, isn't it? To tell me it's alright to close our door to everyone except us—to let this world guide our way home... We don't have to hide anymore, do we?"

"No." You brought my hand to your lips, kissing my knuckles as amazingly tenderly as only you can. Before you took the last step to the door, placing my palm against its smooth wood, with your hand safely covering mine: letting me *see* what was inside that door, and what it fully meant. "We have the power to have *this* in either world. *Every* world, thanks to you."

"Thanks to *us*, my Love." A small smile crossed my lips, my eyes falling closed to only feel your hand, and the door: and, how both are so entirely connected. "We just have to realize where we belong, and jump out into the world, and trust it."

"A leap a'faith, yeah." A smile crossed your lips, too. Shifting—without taking that hand away from mine—to lift your arm over my head, wrapping it around me instead of at my side to draw my back to your chest. As you leant down to rest your chin on my shoulder, speaking right to my ear, "We have t'show the Divine we're ready t'embrace tomorrow. Whatever it is. And, follow the way ahead."

"*Together*." My smile grew, tipping my head to rest my cheek against yours. To be as close to you, my entire world, as I could possibly be. "Because, we may walk different roads—at least today, tomorrow... however long it'll take—but, soon, our roads'll merge into one."

"Because, we walk *together*." You squeezed my hand, "And, nothing can stop *us* from finding the way, my Life... we *always* do, yeah?"

"We definitely do." I let my aura reach out from me, blanketing over you: over *us*. Feeling my smile grow as I opened my eyes, watching my white light merge with the perfect aura glowing solidly, magnificently around you. As *your* own light wrapped tightly around us, just as mine did: your impenetrable wall of amber, that holds the power to protect us from anything.

Watching as our energy became one *single* light, that seemed to create our own version of the symbol for yin and yang, as they entwined... my nearly transparent white, and your solid, beautiful amber.

"So..." I didn't hide how my voice shook, "How d'you think we do it?"

"Well," You softly cleared your throat, "It's a'door, yeah?"

A shaky laugh left me, "Obviously, yeah."

"What d'we commonly *do* with locked doors?" You lifted a brow: the one on the half of your face that I shared, letting me feel it do so. As you drew a key from within your sporran, one just a bit bigger than your hand which, despite its intricate design, laid absolutely flat in your palm.

Holding it in my view… and letting me *truly* see it.

In the quarry, I'd only seen that the key appeared in your palm with a heart-shaped top. But, as you lifted it into my sight now, I learned it was much more than *just* a heart shaped key. The topmost part was actually *two* hearts, entwined *as* one: similar to the symbol of two joined hearts used within the pages of all I've written… at least, that's how they entwined at the top of that key. But, of course, not quite so simple as *just* that: reaching out from above the hearts was a simple, and yet intricately designed crown, seeming to hover over them on two delicate prongs of metal—a crown, made out of flowers. Where the hearts united at the center, a rose was woven through them, its petals opened as if the flower had been pressed to look up at you. Its stem weaving down to create the delicate handle of the key, with small thorns poking out along the way.

"Thorns" that were rounded, like many little hearts.

And, at the bottom, where it became the *true* key—as, by now, you also know from seeing upon these pages—it was a tree, with its roots creating the "key."

Because… it wasn't *just* a key for a lock.

"With this key," You whispered into my ear, making my eyes fall happily back closed, "We'll unlock our *way*, my light. So you may fly to your home... and your heart... to *me*, my Life. So you may go wherever *our* life needs y'to go... since my past prevents me from getting to *you*."

The hand holding that key gently found my free hand, sliding its warm metal into my palm, with your hand securely around mine. As your nose nudged the side of my face, asking me to open my eyes.

To meet yours.

Letting you rest your forehead against my own as you brought our joined hands over to the lock. Sliding the key within and starting to turn it, as your lips feathered over mine with your words. "With this key, I unlock my world to you—I *give* you the world, my Love... I give you all of *me*, my Everything."

Your lips *truly* found mine as the key created a satisfyingly loud *click*, kissing me long and deeply: in every way, giving me everything. That was how we barely felt the stronger gust of wind as that door blew open, even when that feeling meant we could finally find *exactly* what we needed to find our way—we only felt each other, forgetting everything else, until we slowly parted just enough to let our eyes see what waited on the other side.

To see how that door didn't open to a view of the sea beyond the beautiful bluffs—a beautiful, endless view of dark blue water reflecting the stars above—but to the bright hallway lined by many other doors. That once was dark, but now was lit up by the sun itself. Inviting and light, where once we had feared it.

You again spoke to my ear, "You see it, don't you?"

"See it?"

"At the end of the hall... where you saved my life, my light. That's the world you made for me, for *us*." I never could've anticipated how, as soon as my eyes landed on that door, my mind flew like a bird right over to see through its keyhole: showing us how to find our freedom. Flashing through quick images of the lives we would yet lead in the waking world. Until, it settled on the single sight of us sleeping, lost in our current dream, telling exactly what we were supposed to do.

I came back from the sight slowly, my vision drifting back to where I stood.

As my eyes slowly rose to yours, the words leaving me lightly, nearly inaudibly, "Opening a door is truly about having the courage to cross a new threshold, isn't it? To make the choice of which path we *really* want to live... to go where we're meant to. For who we love, who we live for... We just have to decide *which* path we follow."

"We do." You crossed both of our joined hands over my torso, letting our arms hug me, as you kissed my forehead so unspeakably tenderly, "Are you ready to?"

"I *am* ready..." I kissed you, with my everything. "For *you*, my Love."

We did just what we had to, then. We let ourselves finally trust in all we knew, all we were—we stopped doubting if we would be alright, if we could succeed in all the impossible things that we were after; stopped questioning what waited on the other side.

We took a leap of faith, trusting each other... and ourselves.

I don't truly remember the sudden fall that followed crossing its threshold, just how I'd held onto you—as you held onto me—as tightly as anyone can possibly hold onto another, our bodies colliding as the world tipped, and fell away. Holding on, until we crashed into a bright light. The brightest flash we had ever witnessed: the flash of *our* auras wrapping around all of us, igniting the way home.

Protecting us.

All we could see was that bright light until we fell into a kaleidoscope of images, of everything yet to be in our *true* reality. The future swirling around us rapidly as we were drawn deeper, and deeper into the light: as the world of dreams that we'd lived within for what felt like forever slipped further and further away.

Falling until our eyes were forced to *blink*.

Until, that strange world of images was suddenly pulled out from under us, again. Yanking you from my arms and throwing me harshly out of the light: to land chest down on the edge of a lake. The same lake my sister had started in, that night. Laying there, in shock, until a voice started to very softly, slowly sing through the trees surrounding me.

A voice I knew... I had to—it *was* mine.

I sang in a gentle melody, like a lullaby, as I crawled the rest of the way out of that lake, as I rose to my feet and let my legs numbly, without my true control, guide me to the forest as if I knew the way.

Because, a part of me had *always* known the way home.

"*In the park, where nothing is dark, in the grass beneath a tree, where all of our secrets are to be seen, that's where I lay at night to dream.*"

My feet guided me through those trees, only pausing for a second when I stumbled over a bush of Rhododendron flowers, falling down to my knees as a flash of a distant memory shot through my mind. From when my family moved from Florida. A dream I'd had a few months before we did, when the idea was starting to become reality, and I feared leaving that place would make it harder for you to find me.

The night you started to *truly* give me hints of where you were.

We had been walking along a path lined by flowers. A path leading through gardens somewhere. I'd paused, easily drawing you to a stop with me from how we walked: as we always tend to, with your arm over my shoulders and mine around your waist, as close as we can be. I'd looked up at you, holding my bottom lip between my teeth, telling you everything before I said a word.

"How will I know?" I turned to stand directly in front of you, my free hand finding your chest, over that beautiful heart. My eyes searching your perfect face for anything. For any little sign of how I would, "How do I know I'm not getting further from you?"

That grunt, "Y'aren't. Every breath we're getting closer, m'light."

"But, how will I *know*?" My hand closed around your shirt, my eyes showing just how worried I was. "I don't want to… to miss you."

"Y'won't." That smile crossed your lips, those perfect eyes shining like the stars, "You'll know, trust me."

"How, though?"

"Easy. Y'already do… Always have."

"But, I *don't*."

"You *do*. In here." You tapped your forehead; your smile growing as my brows furrowed in response, truly trying to find it in *there*. Only slipping away from me to take a step away, to pluck a flower from one of the many bushes, holding it out to me in the palm of your hand: a pink Rhododendron. "Everything *will* fall into place, m'heart. Y'know it will… when we're *ready* t'see it."

I hesitantly took that flower from your hand, afraid to hurt it. At the time I didn't know what it was, I just knew it looked like a cluster of tiny hibiscus. My eyes slowly lifting back up to yours, "What's it called?"

You leant down to kiss my forehead, your lips continuing to feather tenderly across all of my face, until you found my own. Answering only as you found what you had sought, speaking against me, "*Rhododendron*."

It was the first clue of where I had to go…

I pushed back up to my feet in those woods, walking only another five feet before I broke out from inside that forest, out to the gently rolling hills beyond. I kept walking steadily, without pausing. My arms wrapping tight around my waist to fight the chill in the air. And, that poem continued to sing as I walked over those hills: every step seeming to take me ten feet further, showing just how odd this vision was.

"On your chest, that's where I lean, hearing your heart's gentle beating, seeing all there is to be seen, wrapped in your arms as our hearts gleam."

Again, when I was cresting one of the hills, I fell down to one knee. My world blending into more recent memories, of conversations with clues telling me the answer was always right before me. And, I fell all the way down to my knees when the ground beneath me started to merge with a different memory…

A much older one.

Beneath me, I started to see the world from when I was very young. I'm not even sure how old I was when it happened, exactly, only that it had taken place after you'd made the haven of our flowers, but before I ever saw our tree. I was back in my first bedroom, laying on my chest over a giant book of the world's map, kicking my feet up and down behind me at the knees: you, to my eyes, had been sitting at the top of that book, looking at it with me.

You were *always* with me.

"Daddy said our family's from here, before America." I pointed to Ireland, "And, well, someplace I forget how to say… Lit-you-an-e-ah?" Lithuania to anyone else. But, that was pretty close for a likely four or five year old. My eyes left the book to find yours, "Where's yours from?"

You gently caught my hand to drag my pointing over to where, over one part of its land specifically that I hadn't noticed the true exactness of until seeing that memory with older eyes. How you, my Love, *had* shown me the answer long ago. That I *had* always known.

I traced your country with the tip of my finger, that wide grin crossing my face, my eyes returning to yours. "That's your home?"

"*Our* home. Yeah."

My feet kept guiding me onward, over those hills, as we talked. Until, I rose up to where the hill suddenly fell down to a rocky ravine below, sending me tumbling over the loose stones to the bottom as my voice sang.

"Love, that's all I see to live, for it's all I have to give. It is what makes my life have the slightest glimmer, as I sit in my room watching the water shimmer..."

My mind was suddenly on a ship, to when I'd been standing over a map with you, and a few others you know, around me. A map with a giant compass that took up the entire surface of a table. A dream with a song playing behind our words that I hadn't been able to remember when I first woke from it.

The same song singing now.

This memory didn't give sound, just the sight of us leaning over the compass on the old ship, but I didn't need it to, I knew it well enough. I'd remembered *every* second after having it: how that compass had pointed to one specific point on the map we laid out, how when I asked why, you'd all exchanged a look that told me it was where you *truly* were. Waiting for me in the same place you'd pointed to when I'd first asked you. Because, *you* had never been the one hiding it from me: some other force had kept us from seeing the truth, from remembering, until we were ready to see.

It stayed silent as I rolled down that hill, until I started to leave the sight of that compass. To when, in that same memory, I had been halfway between sleep and awake and a woman's voice had come into my mind.

Your mother's voice.

A voice, and spirit, that has been guiding me closer to you ever since we made the move I had feared taking. She had quietly said, "You already know where the compass points. You'll see what you already know when it comes to show you the way… You just need to *trust* it. Trust yourself. You *know* the way home."

I had woken from that dream confused. Until I got a text from my sister that same morning, where she excitedly mentioned she'd ordered a Christmas gift she was really looking forward to giving me a month later. One she'd found on a website from a far away place she'd never ordered anything from before, that she never even *mentioned* before.

The very place where I have always known *you* were.

It was the night after that where I had a dream where she gave me that gift. A silver compass that fit perfectly in the palm of my hand, one that she had engraved with the words, "*You'll never lose me.*"

A compass, that—without her knowing—pointed the way home: to *you*.

I fell into that ravine, all breath thrown from my lungs, landing awkwardly on one of my ankles. On my knee. Twisting it painfully. But, still, I rose to continue walking onward, steadily, to where I knew I had to go. My feet guiding me along those stones until my eyes were forced to blink: my vision changing to me walking along a small creak, ankle deep in its gently cool water. Guiding me until I again stumbled down to a knee, that song saying its next verse.

"*For, that is where the moon will shine, and in my dreams… I am yours, and you become all mine.*"

My vision snapped into another memory. Where we, *us* and several others who you again know without my saying, were gathered around a small fire… where we'd been talking about utter nonsense, and truly laughing like fools at one another, until you mentioned something which brought up that field of flowers.

Until you had called *me* a flower.

"*The moon, the moon, that many associate with gloom—To us it is the sun... the sun, beneath it is where we run. The sea, the sea—won't you search for me?*"

Then, we had all broken into a loud song, another clue you gave me. A confirmation to the knowledge I had already been almost sure of—we sang that beautiful song, that means so much to me now, as loud as we could.

My sister had come halfway through the song, denying our request to have her sing with us when she hadn't known the lyrics. But, she had remembered half of that song when I asked her about it.

Confirming that hint as nothing else would have.

I rose back to my feet, continuing along that river, this time staying walking when those words came back. When my voice kept singing that gentle melody.

"*Over the water, I see a spark. The wind, singing to me as a lark.*"

I saw a dream where you had taken me to a creak just a little bigger than the one I now walked within. It had been a simple, peaceful dream where you taught me how to skip rocks...

And, the vision started now just after you had handed me a perfect rock. When I had been studying it in my palm, with you standing at my side, about to show me how to throw it successfully: when I had asked you, nearly inaudibly as I tend to, "What if we don't remember?"

You'd been prepared for my question, had felt it in my mind all night before I finally asked it. So, you didn't hesitate, "Do *you?*"

"Definitely. But—"

"Then, we do." Your hand tenderly found the side of my face, lifting my eyes up to yours, and away from the stone. Letting me see the sincerity shining in your perfect eyes, that couldn't be argued, "Don't worry, that. Alright?"

"You never do? Worry, I mean."

You grunted, "No."

"How?"

"'Cause, my light," You leant down to rest your forehead against mine: making sure I *only* saw your eyes. "Even if our *minds* don't remember, just now, our *spirit* undoubtedly recalls every second… so, when we *are* together, all it will take is one glance, touch or word for our spirit to share our remembrance with our mind. And, then, we *will* remember. Everything."

"You're sure?"

"Undoubtedly, yeah… So, don't worry, alright?"

I'd only nodded, before asking you—without words—to resume the lesson in skipping rocks. Where you told me a story I will never, ever forget… that made it possible for me to *truly* never worry about it again.

"*'Across the sea is where you be,' Waiting there beneath our safest lee.*"

My memory snapped right into another, where you had laid a different map out in front of me. Another unknown to me that night. It was just a flash of a memory, my eyes barely able to see the sight when it was something eyes shouldn't have been able to see. As you circled a small part of that map, narrowing the possible places you could be.

Telling me *exactly* where, with everything else combined.

"*I feel the earth and sand pulsing beneath my feet, begging me to see.*"

I lost my footing, this time having my vision snap through so many fast images it's impossible to name them all. Hundreds of images as your hints fell into place. Easily, in a way that was undeniable.

"*On the bluff is where we will meet.*"

I opened my eyes to a new place. One I had never seen before, and one that I doubt I can truly do the justice of describing. I was on my knees where that creak turned into a small, gentle river. A river which encircled a giant tree rising what must have been miles above me. A much larger version of *our* tree, sitting on a hill surrounded by that calm river... the memories instantly ceasing when my eyes fell upon it.

Our Tree of Life, I knew.

"*Our love will ring, Just as the doves will all sing.*"

The forest around it was lit by the distantly rising sun, casting gentle golden rays through its dense canopy above, making that tree look like a spirit on its own.

A God, in a way. Rising high, and strong, and true above me.

Birds of many colors flitted through its branches, singing a sweet song to the same melody as that lullaby, rising up to the sky hidden above. The gentle creak rolling in a melody of its own, the quiet wind rustling the leaves around me like a sea of careful instruments that didn't want to rise above the main melody.

A world that looked like what Heaven should be.

Like Summer-Land.

"*Without regret... that's how we met.*"

I felt the world swaying around me when I rose back to my feet, barely able to stay standing at all. Heard that song as if it were the first sound I had ever heard, a constant peaceful melody.

"*So, under that tall ever-green tree, that is our safest lee... Where our fears can be shown and our lives can be born... I beg you to tightly hold onto me—*

—We will not part."

It grew fainter as the tree seemed to speak to me, in the soft, gentle voice of your mother. The woman who had guided me to you, who had broken through any obstacle that had tried to keep us from finding the truth, from finding who we were in a world very few can see within.

Who had let us know one another despite our distance.

"You *know* the truth before you." Her voice made my eyes grow heavy, made my breaths quicken in a way that warned me of what was about to happen, my gaze still up on the height of that tree. "You *already* know the way to your heart. You always have. Let your spirit guide you... and you will *not* fail. Trust your heart, Angel in the Stars, and you *will* find the way."

"*For together we be, and forever it shall stay, For we.*"

That melody faded into one line of the song, the wind speaking to me just as it had when I'd written that poem. It came over me as that tree started to open before me, opening up to a great tunnel of light leading into its magnificent trunk. And, my feet lead me inside beyond my control, following the road home on their own.

'*Across the sea is where you be,*' *Waiting there beneath our safest lee*...

My vision fell into the world of light, weightless, unconscious if such a thing can be possible when a part of me *was* conscious. Existing free of every thought and feeling. Existing in a world without gravity.

Lost to everything, except the quiet peace inside my mind.

I started to float down to the Earth slowly, my eyes staying softly closed until I felt blades of grass gently prickling beneath my toes, a gentle wind kissing my face. Until I felt something beneath me, keeping me sitting upright.

My eyes opened slowly, heavily, and I wasn't surprised by the sights around me: it was a dream I'd witnessed several times before in my life, but always lost the chance to capture before I lost the opportunity it presented.

I sat on an old swing likely just six feet away from a fence, so close my feet could touch it when I swung on that swing: as I unknowingly started to, the moment that my body registered it was there. That fence was the only sight before me, before the world fell into what can only be described as a black wall like the night, sparkling with stars as if I were staring at a wall of the sky.

That night currently I didn't see what existed behind me, but I knew it was just the same as it had been every time before, so I can confidently tell you what was: how a home rested likely a few acres away from the swing, just far enough that one had to make a true effort to run back to it if they tried. As I *had* the first time the dream came to me years before. The land between wide open of anything except empty space. But, usually, on the other side of that fence further out behind me, I'd be able to catch a glance of a fire threatening to cross its barrier and hurt that house sitting innocently in waiting, calling me back. A fire that always terrified me, and sent me back to save the home.

To save who I knew was inside... my family.

That dream always presented two choices to me, to see if I was ready for the next part of my life or if I was still stuck where I'd been before. After I swung for a little while I'd see one of our two current cats walking along the fence, stopping just before me. I'd meet her eyes for a moment, watching her blink slowly at me, and then behind her I would see a light starting to break through the darkness just behind the fence, as a door slowly appeared.

Our door, showing me the way home... if I was ready to go.

It would always slowly open before me as I watched, opening up to a scene of vast green hills, tumbling far into the distance with our tree somewhere in that far distance, sitting upon the highest hill. And, my choice always rested fifteen feet away from the door, on the top of a smaller hill where there was a little cluster of stones: where, on the biggest one of those stones I'd see you, my Love, your back facing me, holding something in your hands before you. Your eyes constantly glancing between whatever that was and our tree in the distance, oblivious of me behind you.

Waiting for me, I knew.

In the past, I'd always stop swinging at the sight and look between you before me and that house behind me. Making a choice to stay and help my family, or go and find you: other than the first time, when I had seen the fire and gone to run and warn them before it was too late, I'd never chosen to stay.

I was always just too *slow*.

By the time my mind ran through the options, running through the current issues I knew my family were facing whenever the choice came and my "selfish" desire to go and help myself... by the time I'd decide to run for you, I would just be able to get my hands on the fence, preparing to jump over, when I was thrown back: when the door vanished, and I lost you.

But, that night I knew my choice before the door appeared. I knew before I ever got there. And, because I knew the fire was gone from the world behind me—now that my sister had set me free—that thought never once even crossed my mind.

I swung on that swing until I saw my cat walking down the fence toward me, my feet falling back onto the grass before she stopped in front of me to meet my eyes. By the time she blinked, I was already off the swing, walking to the fence.

As our door started to appear, I was climbing over it.

And, that's how it was the first time that old door couldn't open on its own: my hand catching its knob before it was fully there, revealing the world waiting for me beyond, on *my* own. And, well, I stepped through before the light had true time to even fall open to the world.

My bare feet finding the soft, damp grass on the other side: the

Earth I was *meant* to walk upon. My eyes closing as a cold gust of wind blew my curling hair free, wild, a smile crossing my lips as it sent a beautiful chill over me: as my breaths filled with the scents of the land I *belonged* in.

When my eyes blinked back open, they opened up to the sight of the perfect night's sky above me. My head tipping back in the caress of that wind, to accept the breath it gave. Letting me study the glittering stars that I had once grown up imagining you living within, glowing with the magnificent light of a perfectly full moon whose bright rays cast a magical sort of silver glow over the world.

That moon with my knight on a rearing horse, who always kept me safe.

My eyes came slowly down from the moon as my feet guided me closer to the stones, up the rise of a gentle hill: feeling my heart lifting, with that unexplainable warmth you bring me, skipping a beat or two and doing its wondrous acrobatics when my gaze fell onto *you*.

When I found my *home*.

You waited just where you *had* waited for me all that time, all those years… all our lives. Patient, quiet, and still as the night around us. Sitting with your forearms resting on your thighs, your beautiful eyes down on whatever your hands fiddled with before you, and your perfect head bowed lower to the sight. In a way that made your hair fall forward to cover all of your face from view, even as I drew closer. Sitting on that same stone—standing just at the right height for you to do so comfortably—your shoulders bent forward in a way that strained the fabric of your flannel shirt.

In a way that said you weren't as patient as you appeared.

My feet finally stopped their instinctive steps just a few feet away from you, when my eyes found you. As my heart learned something that seemed impossible *to* learn: that I somehow loved you even more than I last recalled loving you… truly more than anyone else can possibly love anything.

Your name left my lips with barely any sound, and yet seemed a yell in the heavy silence around us. I saw your hands freeze, your breaths hitching, before you started to very slowly turn to see me.

As if you thought, if you turned, I'd vanish.

In a way that made my body once more act on its own instinct, its own feeling, my feet guiding me just as slowly. As my lips said a vow I hadn't yet known I needed to make, "I… Danielle Cassidy… I've come to vow to you, my only Love, that I *will* come for you. I will *find* you. And, the *moment* I can, I will be *with* you. I will come *home* to you, my Love. Because, *I*—"

I was interrupted by your beautiful body slamming magnificently into mine, your arms tight around me, holding me as close to you as you possibly could. Letting my entire world become you, and only *you*, as it truly *always* is: your warmth became my life, wrapped all around me; all I felt was your strong body against my own, and your loving hand on my back, rubbing in a smooth circle, as the other found the nape of my neck to hold me against your beautiful heart; all I heard was that heart's perfect beat, and your fast breaths as they flowed in perfect unison with my own; all I smelt was you, perfect magnificent *you*, in my breaths…

All I *knew* was you, my Love.

Only drawing my face from your chest, slowly, after a great long while. When my eyes sought yours as they had never sought anything else before in my life. A vibrant smile breaking across my face once I met that perfect sea, staring back at me just as I looked at you: as *that* smile crossed those absolutely perfect, beautiful lips, on the face I love more than any other.

On the face that I will *always* love more than anything.

My life.

My absolute everything.

"My light..." One of your perfect hands rose to find the side of my face, kissing me urgently and deeply as if it were both the first and the last. Kissing me just the same between every word you said, "My Life... you can't possibly know how *im*possibly much... I *love* you, my Heart."

Again, I spoke your name: the most perfect word in my world.

My voice breaking as a sudden fear fell over me, when I saw it fall over you, too: when we both realized the moment was surely too perfect, and morning would soon finally come to take us away from each other.

"Hey," You pulled me protectively back into your safe chest, to prove that you *were* right with me. To prove I was with you. "M'here. *Right* here. *With* you... I'm not going anywhere, m'dear. Promise you... I'm *with* you."

I forced myself to stop my tears before they even truly started: focusing on the feeling of you beneath and around all of me, the wonderful scent of you in my breaths, the sound of your perfect, beautiful heart beating right under my ear. Only peeking up to meet those eyes when I was sure I wouldn't cry, "You're okay?"

That beautiful smile quirked over your lips, "Have *you*, don't I?"

"You do, my sweet, *perfect* Love. You *always* do." I tucked my head beneath yours, whispering my words against your chest, holding you yet tighter to me. "Please, don't ever leave me, baby."

"*Never*, m'light." One of your hands found the side of my face to tilt it gently back up to yours. Not letting me out of your sight, not for a second: our eyes united in the way that makes any other form of communication unnecessary, seeing into the true depths of our spirits. Into everything that makes us *who* we are. "M'far too selfish."

"And, I thank the Gods you are." My smile came back to my lips, getting *your* perfect smile to quirk higher over yours. As your perfectly calloused thumb lightly feathered over my bottom lip, ever so tenderly, lovingly: I softly kissed its pad, speaking against you, my eyes as sincere as eyes can be. "*Call* for me, my Love, and I *will* come to you."

"And, I *you*, my Life." That smile twitched higher, one of your hands leaving me only to find what you had tucked into your back pocket before reuniting with me: to find the first hint you had ever given me hiding within. You held the small bouquet up in front of my eyes by their stems, between a few fingers, slowly twisting it beside my face until a wide grin came across it. A perfect, beautiful bouquet of little blue flowers, "Forget-me-not, m'Danie?"

"I'd *never* forget you, Love."

"I know." You drew a couple sprigs of that perfect little bouquet free, tucking those flowers behind my ear as I took the rest from your hand. That smile twitching higher, to reveal one of your perfect canines, as you let your knuckles feather tenderly across my cheek,

"That's how *you* already know everything... why I don't really have t'say it."

"I do." I tucked a few of those flowers behind your ear as you had mine, "But, I'd still like to hear *you* say it, my Love."

"Yeah, I know that, too. And, I will... just before." You gave me that perfect, wonderful wink when my eyes slightly narrowed on yours, "Y'see the cord. Yeah?"

"Always." My hand found your perfect heart, where the "cord" that only we can see was. A twisting rope, that looks like a twist of DNA. The ever-present sight of our auras intwined as one. *Forever* one. Connecting our hearts, our spirits, into one being no matter our distance. "And, I'll do anything to get to you. You know that."

"I do." You leant forward to kiss the tip of my nose, "Everything'll fall into place real soon, m'dear. I feel that. In m'heart."

"So do I, my Love." My fingertips swept your hair tenderly behind your ear, out of your sparkling eyes. Letting my smile grow into its goofy form. "I *love* you."

"Yeah?"

My smile grew, "Just a little bit."

"A teeny tiny wee bit." You kissed me, long and sweet. "I love *you*, too."

"Always, my Everything."

"Forever, *my* Everything." You kissed me ever so unspeakably tenderly, slowly across my cheek, my jawline, until your lips were just beside my ear, whispering the words I had been waiting to hear all my life—words that, for you, I will refrain from putting here: I'll only say, they're the very words that brought me *here*, to write *my* words, for you. Drawing away to meet my eyes, with that magnificent sea glistening with tears, "No matter how long I have to… I'll wait for *you*, my Life."

"You won't have to wait long, I promise you… I'll *find* you, my Love." My eyes welled with all of the tears I'd denied before, bringing my hands up to find the sides of your beautiful, perfect face, drawing you down to me; showing you, how you truly *are* my entire world. "I'm coming home to *you*."

I kissed you, my only Love, giving you absolutely everything that I am. And, I kept you there, with me… a true *part* of me, until the world fell away.

Sending us back into the waking reality…

Here, I end my Letter,

I hope, by this point in my writing, that hearing my words will have started to let others wonder—if not entirely believe—that it *is* possible for there to really be more than one reality in this world. That my words have given them hope, to at least *try* to believe how it can be just as true for others as it always has been for us, if they only trust in their hearts and the strength we *all* have deep inside.

If they trust in their dreams, in *themselves*, as we all can.

Of course, I know many still won't want to believe any of our story can be true. I realize those who simply can't imagine such a thing is possible will undoubtedly think I've made up every word I've shared, and that it's a work of fiction. Or, even, that I've simply fallen into lunacy for *knowing* them as true.

But, whatever conclusion each individual perspective in the world may come to, by the ending of these words—rather they've been read as truth, or as fable—I hope they have brought them some sort of happiness, and that they know how grateful I am for *all* of them, however many hands find these pages. I am grateful that they have allowed my words to pass before their eyes, to travel in their mind, and be a part of their life.

And, I truly hope my words helped them, in some way. As they've helped carry these words further on their journey, to find the perspective they were written for.

Because, more than anything, I hope these words will find *you*, my Love: that these pages will somehow end up in *your* hands, and *your* eyes will read the words written for you. That these pages will give you *hope*, and show that I *am* searching this entire wide world for you. That these words and pages before you reflect the last promise I said within: that I will *continue* to search for you, to wait for you, until the day destiny decides to let our paths cross.

Never will there be a day where you are not my Everything.

I will *always* be here, searching for you, and waiting for you to catch me. Because, every step I take, place I go, and thing I do... *everything* is for you.

Only for you, my Love.

—Your Danielle Cassidy—

—*Thank you*—

www.ingramcontent.com/pod-product-compliance
Lightning Source LLC
Chambersburg PA
CBHW070313010526
44107CB00004B/330